COMPLETE HMO
PROPERTY SUCCESS

THE PROVEN STRATEGY FOR FINANCIAL FREEDOM FROM MULTI-LET PROPERTY INVESTING

by Nick Fox

with Richard Leonard

ISBN: 978-0-9935074-0-3

First published in England in 2016 by Fox Print Partners

COMPLETE HMO PROPERTY SUCCESS

THE PROVEN STRATEGY FOR FINANCIAL FREEDOM FROM MULTI-LET PROPERTY INVESTING

by Nick Fox

with Richard Leonard
published by Fox Print Partners

Contents

HMO PROPERTY RENOVATION & REFURBISHMENT SUCCESS

NEXT STEPS....

For my family, friends and business partners.
You all inspire me daily. Thank you.
Nick

About the author

A prolific and highly successful investor, Nick Fox has been involved with property since his early childhood. Today, his investment portfolio includes more than 200 buy to let properties – both shared accommodation and single household lets – and he has interests in a number of development projects.

As is the case with so many successful businesspeople, Nick started young. When he was eight, he bought up all the penny sweets from the Scout Camp tuck shop and sold them on to his friends for 2p! His delight at doubling his money on his first business venture signposted an entrepreneurial attitude and launched an enthusiasm for making money on his own terms that has never left him.

His introduction to the property market came not long afterwards, when the caravan that he lived in with his mother burned down. She used the insurance money to buy a wreck of a house, which she did up and sold for a profit, repeating the process until they had a nice home. When he wasn't in school, Nick helped his mother out and began to understand not only what could be achieved by hard work, but also the potential of property as a money-making vehicle. He just needed a bit of capital to get him started.

In 1988, at the age of 19, Nick landed a job with a company that imported computer software from America and sold it into retailers in the UK. It didn't take long for Nick to see the technology boom that was starting and he quickly realised he could do the same thing himself.

Operating out of his bedroom, Nick took out as many credit cards as he could and bought software stock from all over the world. He started off selling into small retailers, then, when the market for personal computers really took off, he moved into proper premises and grew the company until it became the UK's leading budget software company, selling over a million units every month into Dixons, Woolworths and WHSmith.

But by 2002 business had peaked. Technology had gone mainstream and was even available in supermarkets, and things quickly declined for Nick.

2005 was the 'light bulb' moment, when he realised that the income from his various businesses might have paid for his lifestyle, but it was his home that had built equity and given him a lump-sum return. He knew that the quickest and only way he could replace his financial losses was to buy more properties.

By the end of 2005, Nick had five properties, all rented to friends, generating an income and building equity. He started buying larger homes, which he rented as single units to families, and by the end of the following year, Nick had 20 properties and a significant buy to let business.

In 2007, he went into a buying frenzy. Within 12 months, he'd added another 90 properties to his portfolio. Then, as the credit crunch hit and many of his mortgages moved off initial low fixed rates and onto variables, Nick started to look at how he could increase his profits and turned one of his existing family home lets into an HMO. That was light bulb moment number two.

He began to partner with other investors and subsequently doubled the size of his portfolio to more than 200 properties, around 100 of them HMOs. That portfolio is currently managed through the Milton Keynes letting agency he set up in 2010 and achieves 98% occupancy.

"Everyone thinks I must be constantly working to keep so many plates spinning but, really, I just employ great managers and develop effective systems."

Nick's HMO investment strategy is now highly regarded within the industry and he is regularly asked to speak at property investment events. His expertise is called on by new clients and fellow professional investors alike and his reputation has enabled him to establish a significant mentoring business.

Over the past few years, Nick has also acquired business interests outside property: a photography company that he's looking to franchise and investment in a local pre-school that serves 80 children and has been rated 'outstanding' by OFSTED.

Nick loves football, tennis, golf and boating and has climbed Mount Snowdon with his partner, Samantha. He is committed to supporting local charitable causes and is also a Patron of Peace One Day. He and Samantha live just outside St Albans with their five children.

Author's disclaimer

I am not qualified to give financial or legal advice. All related recommendations made in this book should only be considered in consultation with suitably qualified and accredited professionals. Persons giving financial advice MUST be properly qualified and regulated by the Financial Services Authority (FSA) and anyone giving you legal advice should be suitably qualified and regulated by The Law Society and the Solicitors Regulation Authority (SRA) (or the Council of Licensed Conveyancers (CLC)).

A note from Nick…

This compilation brings my two HMO-focused books together as one. There is a little duplication of information but I have left it all in, as it maintains the flow of each book and the content is written in slightly different ways. Plus, a little revision never hurts, so stick with it!

And the fourth part: NEXT STEPS gives you the opportunity to get hold of some free stuff – a good reason to read right to the end!

I hope you enjoy this 'HMO superbook' and do get in touch if you have any questions or would like some advice from me, personally. We're here to help.

EMAIL hello@nickfox.co.uk
TEL 01908 930369
FACEBOOK Nick Fox Property
TWITTER @NickFoxMentor

Also by Nick Fox:

The Secrets of Buy to Let Success

Property Investment Success

Complete Property Investment Success

101 Top Tips for Property Investment Success

Available in paperback from nickfox.co.uk & Amazon.co.uk
Audiobook available from Amazon.co.uk and Audible.co.uk
Kindle and iBook formats also available

HMO PROPERTY SUCCESS

THE PROVEN STRATEGY FOR FINANCIAL FREEDOM FROM MULTI-LET PROPERTY INVESTING

Introduction

This book is about cash-positive investing in Houses in Multiple Occupation and is aimed at those of you looking to generate on-going monthly income. It won't tell you everything you need to know – this is not intended to be an exhaustive manual! – I'm simply trying to give you a picture of what's involved in building an efficient HMO business and becoming a successful investor.*

Financial freedom means different things to different people; to me it means having the reassurance that, even if I stopped working tomorrow, the level of income generated by my HMO portfolio is sufficient to not only pay the bills, but also provide my family with a good quality of life for the foreseeable future. Everyone's financial requirements are different, so when I say I'm giving you a proven strategy for achieving financial freedom, what I'm doing is showing you how to secure excellent returns from buy to let and you can take that to whatever level you want and/or need. For some people, three or four properties will mean financial freedom; others may need a portfolio of ten or more.

Lastly, just before we get started, something that I don't hear property investors talking about enough is the importance of having supportive family and friends, so that's something I want to stress to you. It will be nigh-on impossible for you to succeed in this business if the people around you aren't understanding and encouraging, because becoming a professional property investor is like any other start-up business - there are peaks, troughs, exciting times and times when you just need to get your head down and push through. But I promise you, and you can promise them: it's worth it.

As my most wise and successful mentor once told me:

Leap and the net will appear.
Take action now...

*The caveat to the blueprint for HMO success that I talk about is that it's very hard to make the model work in London, where the property price / rental income ratio is generally much higher than in the rest of the country.

"Never allow yourself to become one of those people who, when they are old, tell you how they missed their chance."

Claire Ortega, Author

PART ONE:

UNDERSTANDING

YOUR INVESTMENT

Chapter 1

Why do you want to invest?

When I first began investing, I was pretty sure property was a sensible choice because I knew it was an asset class that could provide me with on-going income while appreciating in value to make a nice pension pot for the future. That was in the 'noughties', when the market was booming and buying property was easy, so I simply went out and bought what I knew would rent profitably. What I didn't do until a year or so later was take those vague notions of 'income' and 'pension' and start to make some real sense of them.

It's impossible to make the right investment decisions unless you have sat down and clearly established the financial and lifestyle motivators behind your desire to invest. Property is only 'a sensible choice' if it delivers on your objectives, suits your attitude to risk and personality, works for your lifestyle and – importantly – you understand that it is a business. Far too many people have ploughed their capital into bricks and mortar with barely a second thought and ended up with something that simply makes their lives a misery.

If you don't go about it in the right way, investing in HMOs can be incredibly challenging, time-consuming and labour-intensive. The potential financial rewards certainly make it worthwhile, but only if you're able to set up and manage a system to effectively run your portfolio as a real and profitable business.

I was lucky that when I bought my first few properties the market was rising and it was so easy to essentially buy 'no money down' – I don't think I would have got away with being so relatively unprepared today. In the current economic climate, and at a time when regulation and availability of financing and refinancing is so much tighter, investing in property is a very different thing and, to be truly successful, there's a great deal of work to be done before you even peer in an estate agent's window. And it all begins with *why* you want to invest.

Your goals

What effect do you want property investment to have on your life? A lot of people talk about becoming 'financially free' through property, but the exact definition of that is different for everyone, depending on their current situation, expectations and desires. You need to make a clear list of exactly what you need and want your investment to give you – financially and in terms of lifestyle – and make each item time-specific. It's been proven that the more detailed you can make your goals, the more likely you will be to achieve them, so it really is worth spending time on this.

> *"Setting goals is the first step in turning the*
> *invisible into the visible."*
> **Tony Robbins**

If you want income, the key questions you need to ask and answer are: how much and by when? I'm sure you've heard of SMART as a tool for setting goals, and it's certainly a good way to check you're thinking in the right way. Look at each item on your list and make sure it's Specific, Measurable, Attainable, Relevant/Rewarding and Time-bound. So, in the case of income, you might put: 'I will be generating £5,000 monthly income from property within the next 2 years, so I can send my child to private school.' It's important that you're realistic (you're not going to make a million in a year!), but at the same time, don't be afraid to dream big.

> *"A vision is a clearly-articulated, results-oriented*
> *picture of a future you intend to create. It is*
> *a dream with direction."*
> **Jesse Stoner Zemel**

And people always achieve their goals more quickly if they're motivated by emotion, rather than purely by money, so try to attach some kind of personal element to each one.

Some people make the mistake of leaving out some lifestyle goals, because they think their ideas sound a bit silly or aren't that important, but this is about you, nobody else, and if you want it, write it down. And write it as though you've already achieved it – don't allow for the possibility of failure! For example:

In 6 months' time…

I spend the whole of every Sunday with my family

I have a massage once a week

My wife has the 4x4 she wants

…and then you can work out the income and time freedom you'll need to generate in order to realise those goals.

Once you know where you want/need to be in the next 6 months, year, 3 and 5 years, you can start to break that down into shorter periods of time and set the weekly (or even daily) targets you need to hit in order to stay on track to achieve your goals.

A good device for illustrating your goals and staying motivated is a vision board – and not just one. My home is full of them, ranging in size from A4 magnetic ones stuck to the fridge door to huge 8x4 foot boards that cover entire walls! I'm a big believer in the power of visualisation and I and my family sees the results and benefits of it every day.

"The future you see is the future you get."
Robert G Allen

Why property?

I've already said that I chose to invest in property because it gives me an income and a pension pot, but it's more than that. It suits my lifestyle, work ethic, skills, risk profile, personality, tax situation and inheritance plans for my children – and these are all things you need to consider carefully.

I'm not a wealth or financial advisor and couldn't even begin to start breaking down the pros and cons of property for every possible circumstance. You need to find financial professionals who can advise you properly and I'll talk more about that in Chapter 6. For now, I would simply say that you will need some significant capital behind you if you're serious about building a portfolio (I'd suggest at least £50,000 for each property you intend to buy) and I'd stress the importance of speaking to a wealth advisor. They can look at all your financial interests and plans for the future and help you decide the best way to invest in property to suit your own, personal situation – and whether property is even the right investment vehicle for you.

What I *can* do is explain why *I* chose property. Quite simply, it offers the most reliable, tangible, flexible, profitable form of investment I've been able to find, and I can break that down into six key aspects:

1. **Leverage:** No other asset class offers the opportunity to leverage in the way that property does. Banks and building societies lend against property at the level they do because property is seen as having a fundamental 'bricks & mortar' value. Markets peak and trough but a property will almost always hold a certain level of value, so while maximum Loan to

Value rates may fluctuate (in the past 8 years, I've seen them fall from 125% to 60% and go back to 85%), you can still leverage other people's money to make a better return on capital than you might otherwise – i.e. you can make your money go further. For example, if there was a 15% rise across all markets:

£100k invested in stocks = £15k growth
£100k invested in £25k deposits on 4 properties, each worth
£100k = £60k growth

2. **Refinancing:** The ability to refinance a property, as an extension to leverage, means you can end up with an income-producing asset that has none of your own capital tied up in it. You can't achieve this as quickly and easily as you once could, but if you manage to buy a property at a good price and that particular sector of the market rises sufficiently, you should be able to remortgage in time and release the money you originally invested. By reinvesting that money in another income-producing property, you're expanding your portfolio and maximising the return on your capital.

3. **Income:** With all other asset classes, you mainly profit from growth on the capital. Although there may be interest payments on other types of investment, I haven't found any that offer the same income potential as property.

4. **Control:** Unlike most other forms of investment, such as stocks or bonds, you have a high degree of control over the investment returns a property provides. While you can't control either the property market as a whole or mortgage rates, you do have the power to decide:

- the type of property you buy
- what mortgage product you have
- how you let the property
- the type of tenants you accept
- the rent you charge (to a certain extent)
- how much you spend on managing and maintaining the property

Essentially, you have a high degree of control over income and expenditure, and, therefore, profitability.

5. **Opportunity:** The diversity of opportunity to make money from property is really exciting to me, and one of the reasons it's used by so many people as a wealth creation tool. Whether you want on-going income, short/medium-term gain, a pension plan, a home for your children in years to come or a lump sum return in the future, property can work for you. You can buy to let single or multiple occupancy units; renovate a property and then sell or remortgage; self build or develop yourself; strike a deal to sell property or land

to a developer; get paid for sourcing property; do everything yourself and make it your career, or work with other people to make it a more passive investment… It really does offer a huge variety of options – even one property can allow you to realise different returns at different times in your life, depending on what you need and when.

6. **Systemisation:** This is a big part of why property works as an investment vehicle for me. If you can put the right systems and team in place to effectively source, acquire, refurbish, let and manage a portfolio, you can reap considerable financial rewards for relatively little of your own time. That frees you up to either focus on high-value aspects of your business, or simply to enjoy some of your lifestyle activities. I said earlier that property is a business, and you need to have the ability to establish and manage a 'head office' in a way that works for you. But as long as you can do that, your systemised business should be able to function as a money-earner whether you're there or not.

I have over 20 people working for me, including a PA, a bookkeeper, a property manager, two lettings negotiators and a maintenance team of more than ten contractors. They take care of my income-generating portfolio, while I spend my time looking for new HMO deals and work on other property-related opportunities.

It's good systemisation that's accelerated the growth of my property business and allowed me to pursue other interests – lifestyle and business - in a way that would otherwise be impossible.

> *"90% of all millionaires become so through owning real estate (property)."*
> **Andrew Carnegie**

Is property right for *you*?

As well as speaking to wealth and tax specialists to help decide whether property is an appropriate investment vehicle from a financial perspective, there are a number of things you need to consider on a more personal level. Investing in high income-generating properties – i.e. HMOs – may suit your financial plans, but…

…are you equipped with the skills to either run an HMO portfolio yourself or effectively manage the outsourcing?

Are you:

- Computer & internet savvy?
- A good administrator?
- Organised?
- Motivated?
- Good at time management?
- Able to employ and manage a team of staff?
- Surrounded by a good personal support network?

…is your attitude to risk in line with the fact that property is considered a medium to high-risk investment? Can you accept having millions of pounds of mortgage debt?

...do you have the people skills to build relationships with other property professionals?

...do you have the appropriate general business skills to succeed?

...do you understand financing and how to put together a business plan?

...will the demands on your time – which are considerable in the first two or three years of building a portfolio – suit your lifestyle?

...can you project manage? You can outsource renovation and refurbishment management to a certain extent, but you still need to understand all the elements and be able to manage the overall project.

If this is the first time you've run your own business, you must understand and be prepared for the highs and lows you'll experience in the first few years. Read as many books as you can about start-up businesses and entrepreneurs - Seth Godin's 'The Dip' is a good one to start with - and you'll see that most of them share the same pattern of successes and challenges, and most have failed at some point. To give yourself the best chance of success, I'd recommend that you keep finding out about people who've already succeeded and learn from their mistakes.

"Anyone who stops learning is old, whether at twenty or eighty. Anyone who keeps learning stays young."
Henry Ford

I read at least one book a week to help keep my mind and business on track – and they're by no means all related to property. Some of the books that are broadly considered 'personal and professional development' tools are exceptionally good; some are, frankly, pretty bad, but there's always something that you can learn from even the poorer ones. You can find a list of the ones that I've found particularly helpful – quite a few of which I've read several times - at the end of this book and also on hmopropertysuccess.co.uk.

But I'd say that the best measure of whether you're suited to property investment is the feedback you get from other investors. Spend some time with other people who are already doing what you want to do, talk to them about their property business, see for yourself what's involved in making a success of it and ask yourself whether you can see elements of yourself in them. People have different approaches and not every investor has the same temperament, personal manner, background or goals, but all of them will probably be:

- self-confident
- committed
- hard-working
- self-motivated
- self-improvers
- people who enjoy business
- good listeners
- good negotiators
- well-supported by friends and family

You'll probably have to pay for their time – and almost certainly to access the best – but it'll be money well spent, I promise you.

"Business and making money are not so much about what happens to you, or the rules that are out there, but your attitude, perseverance, and desire to succeed."
Dolf de Roos

Checklist

Is property investment right for you?

Have you done all these things?

Goals
- ☐ Listed financial and lifestyle goals
- ☐ Checked goals have SMART attributes
- ☐ Made some kind of visual illustration to keep you focused and motivated

Investment options
- ☐ Spoken to a wealth manager / financial advisor
- ☐ Considered which type of property investment will suit your goals
- ☐ Identified capital you can access to fund acquisition and refurbishment

Property as a business
- ☐ Understood the potential risks and rewards
- ☐ Considered skills required to run a business
- ☐ Compiled and committed to a reading list
- ☐ Spent a day with more than one successful investor

Once you've clarified exactly why you want to invest and established that property is the right investment choice to help to realise your goals, you need to look at HMO property investment in more detail.

Chapter 2

The HMO model

HMO (āch'ĕm-ō') n. Abbreviation for House in Multiple Occupation: a property shared by at least 3 tenants, forming more than 1 household*, where the tenants share toilet, bathroom or kitchen facilities.
(as defined by www.gov.uk)

(*A household consists of either a single person or members of the same family who live together. It includes people who are married or living together and people in same-sex relationships.)

Investing in HMOs is by far the best way to maximise rental income and monthly profit from buy to let. There are some exceptions – such as luxury homes and corporate lets in capital cities – but, by and large, buying properties in areas where rental accommodation is in high demand (see Chapter 5) and letting the rooms to individual tenants will generate two to three times the amount of rental income that you could achieve by letting it as a single unit. Yes, the associated costs are higher and it takes more work to manage, but the rental income certainly makes the extra effort worthwhile.

To give you an example… By the start of 2007, I had a decent-sized portfolio of properties, but all were let as single units and, while the portfolio as a whole was profitable, one four-bedroom detached house was losing me money each month. It was a lovely property, so, rather than simply cutting my losses and selling, I decided to create two extra bedrooms and turn it into a six-bedroom HMO. The rental income jumped from £1,200 to £2,500 a month and the liability in the portfolio suddenly become its most profitable asset. That was my 'light-bulb' moment, when I realised how much more profitable my portfolio could be.

Just a little word of warning: if you're now thinking of doing the same to an existing portfolio, stagger the conversions. While it was, ultimately, undoubtedly the right move to turn 20 of my properties into HMOs, what I didn't quite think through was the practicality of doing all 20 at the same time! I think I was so overcome with excitement that I'd 'discovered' this brilliant new business model, that I didn't properly think through the logistical or financial implications. Having all those properties not generating any income for nearly two months, on top of the cost of the necessary refurbishment, meant things were very tight – not to mention hectic - for quite a few months. I'd certainly take my time if I did it again!

A lot of people still think of HMOs as 'student housing', but the model has come a long way in the last ten years and the vast majority of both already successful and new investors I meet are letting rooms to young adults in full-time employment. Some fall into the 'young career professionals' category; others are working in bars, restaurants and shops. Many are on short-term contracts and find it much more convenient to rent a room than a flat for a few months, as landlords usually request a 12-month rental commitment; some tenants will rent a room in the same property for years.

As the landlord of an HMO, you are typically responsible for:

*   providing and maintaining all fixtures, fittings and white goods
*   fully furnishing the property – including kitchen/dining equipment, but not linen
*   paying council tax and utility bills (excluding telephone)
*   providing and paying for broadband
*   providing a regular cleaning service for the communal areas

…in other words, you're providing the kind of accommodation your tenants might expect if they were living at home with their parents – in some cases, better accommodation! The tenants seem to like the ease of all-inclusive rent and, because many of them are of a similar age, it's often a good social environment for them. (See Chapter 9 for more detailed information on refurbishment and getting a property 'ready to rent'.)

The cons

I'm going to start with the downsides, or the more challenging aspects of operating HMOs, because there's no getting away from them and if you're going to get into this business, you need to understand exactly what lies ahead.

Bad press. One of the things you'll always come up against is the preconception that multi-let houses mean cheap and nasty accommodation, run by landlords who care more about making money than the wellbeing of their tenants – packing as many people as they can into one house for the sake of profit. Like it or not, there's a popular feeling out there that 'decent' landlords let properties as one unit, rather than room by room, and choosing to go down the HMO route is rather unsavoury.

Unfortunately, yes, there are some landlords who don't comply with either property regulations or their legal and moral obligations to their tenants, don't look after their investments, and, as the standard of accommodation goes down, so does the quality of tenants. And, because of the media's love of a good horror story, it's these tales of 'slum landlords' and tenants treating properties like 'doss houses' and running cannabis factories that people hear about.

So, although the kind of HMOs I'm talking about running are nothing like that, nor the old stereotype of 'student accommodation' and, thankfully, the number of good, professional landlords is increasing, you need to be prepared for a less-than-enthusiastic reaction when you tell people what you're doing. My advice is to talk as little as possible about it until you're up and running, because it's very easy to be put off by 'advice' from people who have very little relevant understanding or experience.

Heavy management demands. Ask any investor not currently investing in HMOs why they're not, and the first thing out of their mouth will probably be, "It's far too much hassle dealing with all the tenant problems." A group of unrelated people living in a house together can sometimes result in more disagreements and more (often petty) complaints, and you'll undoubtedly get far more maintenance issues than you would renting an unfurnished property to a family. You need tact, diplomacy, strength of character, a good team of tradesmen and the willingness and ability to respond quickly to issues.

Admin. With multiple tenants come multiple sets of paperwork and an increased number of phone calls, viewings, move-ins and move-outs.

Tighter legal requirements. HMOs fall under very specific licensing, planning, health and safety, building and letting regulations and laws. There has been a lot of change in policy over recent years, so you need to make sure that you not only adhere to the policies and requirements in force at the time you acquire and let your HMO, but that you stay up to date and compliant. (See Chapter 3 for more details.)

Staff. If you want to build a significant portfolio of HMOs, there's no question you'll need to employ a team of people to help you run it. You could probably manage between two and five houses on your own, but after that, it can quickly become a full-time job. And going back to why you want to invest, I bet, 'because I want to be a property manager' wasn't anywhere on your list! So you'll need to be prepared and able to hire and manage staff of your own.

The good news is that, while all this is time-consuming and requires organisation and attention to detail, it can all be systemised and outsourced to a small team, under your control. I'll stress again that you must understand this is a property **business** and you'll need business skills to run it.

The pros

The upsides of investing via the HMO model echo the key reasons I gave in the last chapter for why I invest in property as an asset class. To reiterate, HMOs offer the most reliable, tangible and profitable form of investment I've been able to find.

CASH FLOW! I haven't met a single investor who's operating HMOs for any reason other than cash flow and profit! HMOs involve far more work and the running costs are higher than for single lets, but the rental income is up to three times as much as you would get from letting the property as a single unit. That means both your yield and profitability tend to be significantly higher than average buy to let figures. Two reasons why the cash flow is so good are:

a. Voids don't have the same impact as with single lets.
As a general rule of thumb, in an average 6-bedroom HMO, rooms 1 to 4 cover your costs and rooms 5 and 6 are your

profit. The likelihood of having more than one room empty at a time is extremely low, so even if you lose a tenant, you're still profitable, compared to losing a tenant in a single let, which results in you having to cover the property costs yourself – every time.

b. Virtually recession-proof rental income. When times are hard, people cut costs and an all-inclusive room rental makes it easy for people to budget and much cheaper and less hassle than renting a whole flat. I haven't suffered any drop in tenant demand since the credit crunch hit and have consistently operated at 98% occupancy.

Flexibility of investment. Because HMOs tend to be larger properties, the building usually offers the potential to be reconfigured as/when the demand (for rental or sale) changes. Most of the HMOs I've bought have been family houses that I've then reconfigured, by way of stud walls and adding bathroom facilities, so they could easily be turned back into family homes if there was a high demand for those. Similarly, there may be the option to separate the house into separate flats or adapt it to accomodate those with disabilities or the elderly. Buying things that offer a good degree of flexibility means you give yourself the best chance of maximising profitability into the future.

Helping with the housing shortage. Most investors I know have an element of philanthropy in their overall life plan and, while I'm not for a minute claiming to be investing purely for the good of others, the simple fact is that by providing good quality accommodation and maximising the occupancy potential of some of the existing housing stock, we're helping. The Government needs more good, private sector landlords offering decent, affordable housing.

Key Performance Indicators (KPIs) for HMOs

I'll cover KPIs further in Chapter 13, but here are the headlines, for now. Whether you're running a portfolio of HMOs or single-let properties, you have to be able to monitor and measure your investment against itself, other similar properties in the market and other investment options. You need to set up a system – I do it on Excel spreadsheets - to track income and expenditure, rental and capital values and occupancy figures. Those will allow you to assess your returns and see whether you're maximising those returns.

You need to be absolutely precise about the costs and rental income for each property. While that's something your bookkeeper should take care of for you on an on-going basis, you must be able to calculate for yourself - with a high degree of accuracy - how profitable a property is likely to be, BEFORE you buy it. There are a lot of costs associated with buying and operating an HMO and you need a spreadsheet that breaks those down in detail so you can quickly calculate whether the monthly cash flow stacks up and how good a return you'll be getting on the capital you'll need to invest.

Returns can be measured in a number of ways, but I focus on three in my business: profit, return on investment (ROI) and yield.

Profit

Fundamentally, this is what keeps me, my lifestyle and my portfolio going – and I presume it's your main reason for going down the HMO route. In addition to monthly bills, you'll need to plough some of the rental income back into your investment, in the shape of maintenance and updates to fixtures, furnishings and the fabric of the property itself, but you should be building those costs into your budget, so that your 'profit' figure is, or could be, personal income.

Remember to include tax in your costings and revisit all the items on your income and expenditure spreadsheet on at least a monthly basis. Even small reductions in utility bills, a quarter of a percent reduction in mortgage interest and minor increases in rent can add up to a significant increase in profit across a portfolio of properties.

ROI

Annual Profit ÷ Total Capital Invested
= Annual Return On Investment

As a professional investor, ROI should be right up there with profit as a key measure. If your main investment goal is monthly income, you may be tempted to put more capital into your HMO in order to reduce your mortgage payments, but I don't think that's a smart move. I've already said that one of the main benefits of investing in property (versus other assets) is that you can leverage the bank's money and benefit from capital growth on not just your own money, but theirs as well. Investing as little of your own money as possible means that you'll be maximising the return on your own capital – essentially making your money work harder for you.

One of the main benefits of renting out rooms is that the rental income (and therefore profit) is maximised, so you can afford to gear highly. In time, you may be able to refinance so that there is less of your own capital left tied up in the property. If you're able to take all of the original capital out, you'll have an 'infinite' ROI: all the profit for no financial investment.

Example:

Annual rental income	£30,000
Annual costs	£18,000
Annual profit	£12,000
Total capital invested	£75,000
(deposit, buying costs, refurbishment, furnishing, etc.)	
Annual ROI	16% (£12k ÷ £75k)

Refinance after 5 years, withdrawing £50,000, to leave only £25,000 capital invested:

Annual ROI	48% (£12k ÷ £25k)

You can also add capital growth figures to rental income to gain an ROI figure for a period of time, e.g.

Original purchase price	£200,000
Capital invested	£75,000

Value after 5 years	£250,000
Capital growth	£50,000
Rental profit	£60,000 (£12k x 5 years)
Total profit over 5 years	£110,000
Annual ROI over life of investment	29.3% ((£110k ÷ 5) ÷ £75k)

Once you have your ROI figure/s, you can compare it/them to other investment returns and see how your HMOs are performing for you.

Yield

This is talked about as a headline figure by the media and many investors but, for me, it comes behind profit and ROI, and is simply an indication of how 'good' my investment choice is for the area. There are two key reasons why I don't rate it as highly as the other two as a measure of success:

a. National yield figures are usually either gross or don't even state whether they're gross or net – i.e. costs are often not factored in. And sometimes a figure stated as 'net' actually only takes into account the mortgage repayment, none of the other associated costs.

b. Yield doesn't take into account how much of your own capital has been invested, i.e. whether you're highly geared or own the property outright, your yield figure could be the same.

People calculate yield in slightly different ways, but the most common calculations are: rental income divided by the property's value (gross yield), and profit divided by the property's value (net yield).

To use the figures from the last example:

Purchase price	£200,000
Rental income	£30,000
Profit (income – costs)	£12,000 (£30k - £18k)
Gross yield	15% (£30k ÷ £200k)
Net yield	6% (£12k ÷ £200k)

The national average yield figure quoted tends to fluctuate between 4% and 5% - this is mainly based on single lets and is usually a gross figure. As a general rule, HMOs gross between two and three times the national average yield and your net yield percentage should still outstrip the national gross.

Although a lot of the KPI data can be compiled by your property manager and bookkeeper as your business grows, you will have to be able to do it all yourself in the early days. I'd suggest that if you're not already familiar with this kind of data compiling and tracking, that you read some basic business administration books and make sure you understand how spreadsheet programs such as Excel can help you.

The most important thing with analysis and tracking tools is that you understand them and they're user-friendly for you; what's perfect for one investor isn't necessarily the right format for another. Work out a system that suits you, so you can keep it up to date and won't waste time completing information that's not useful to you.

Make it personal

Remember that this is *your* business. The key KPIs listed above are, in my opinion, the most important ones that will enable you to monitor and compare your investment, but there may be others that you'd like to add, according to your fundamental goals and objectives. KPIs don't have to simply be financial, so if spending more time with your children is something you'd like property investment to facilitate, then make that measurable and put it on your spreadsheet. Because if you're succeeding financially, but not in terms of lifestyle goals, it needs to be flagged up and put right as soon as possible. Regular KPI analysis will keep not only your business, but also YOU on track.

Checklist

Understanding the HMO model

Have you done all these things?

- ☐ Understood the difference between student HMOs and renting rooms to working adults
- ☐ Appreciated the downsides and really considered whether you're able and prepared to deal with them
- ☐ Considered again whether the 'pros' will satisfy your goals and objectives
- ☐ Read business administration books/guides and researched KPIs
- ☐ Become familiar with Excel, or a similar spreadsheet program
- ☐ Thought about the type of KPIs you'll need to track in YOUR business

Chapter 3

The financials

Choosing how to finance your HMO investments is a major decision. There are various different options that you'll hear people talking about – great mortgage deals, joint ventures, lease options, etc. – but, fundamentally, which route you take will depend on four key factors:

1. How much capital you have
2. The bank's willingness to lend to you
3. Your attitude to risk
4. Your ability to find the right people and build good relationships with them

Before I go any further, I need to make one thing very clear: 'No money down' (NMD) deals **do not exist**. They used to, but regulations have tightened since the credit crunch hit and I haven't found a single NMD scheme since that is considered legal.

You cannot buy a property solely in your name without putting some of your own capital in and, if you don't fully disclose to a lender where the deposit funds are coming from, you are committing mortgage fraud.

It's also mortgage fraud to not advise the lender of the **actual price** you're paying for the property (which is what some NMD schemes rely on), so if anyone suggests that to you, walk away from them. I'm amazed at how many people I meet who still think they can invest in property without any personal investment of money or time. Thankfully, the number of companies and self-proclaimed 'gurus' out there suggesting it's possible seems to have fallen over recent years, but there are still quite a few rogues looking to take what little money people do have and give them little or nothing in return.

You need money behind you to invest in buy to let. As a rule of thumb, for every HMO you buy, you should budget for:

- a 25% deposit
- purchase costs of around £2,500 (solicitor's fees, disbursements, surveyor, etc.)
- Stamp duty of 1% of the purchase price (if purchase price is £250,000 or less; it's 3% if over £250,000 and 4% if over £500,000)
- somewhere between £5,000 and £30,000 for refurbishment (if required) and getting it ready to rent
- A 'contingency fund' to cover up to 2 months' initial mortgage payments and any other unexpected costs

So, if you're buying at £200,000 (a pretty average purchase price), you're going to need somewhere between £50k and £70k.

This is not a business for the under-funded; it is a major investment and carries risk. The rewards are potentially very good, but it's certainly not something you should enter into lightly and that's why you need to work with a great team of professional advisors. Whoever you choose to help and advise you with financing (broker or IFA), should work together with your legal representative and wealth manager to make sure that what you buy and how you buy it is appropriate for your circumstances and in line with your objectives.

Risk

Property is considered a medium-risk investment, with the risk reducing the longer you plan to hold the investment for. HMO investing in particular offers the potential for great rewards, but with that comes greater risk.

"Progress always involves risks. You can't steal second base and keep your foot on first."
Frederick B. Wilcox

Getting a good ROI means taking on a lot of mortgage debt; having the right business structure in place to run your HMO portfolio involves employing and being responsible for other people; you stake your reputation on every deal you make and, if you choose to partner with another investor on joint ventures, you're not only risking your own money, but theirs as well. It all amounts to a lot of financial and emotional pressure and you need to seriously think about whether you're happy to accept that level of risk and responsibility.

The ultimate level of risk is massively reduced if you approach everything in a professional way, research and execute all your choices properly and become an excellent business manager. In short, it's up to you and dependent on the kind of person you are. If you're confident in your own abilities and are prepared to work hard at this business, you shouldn't need to worry unduly about the risks you're taking, because you'll know that you're doing everything possible to mitigate those risks.

> *"Risk comes from not knowing what you're doing."*
> **Warren Buffett**

Key financial risk factors and how you can insulate yourself against them:

Risk: capital values (house prices) going down.
Mitigate by: buying property at 10%+ below its 'true market'/ surveyed value and considering it a long-term investment.

Risk: rents falling.
Mitigate by: buying in areas where demand is currently high and likely to be high into the future.

Risk: void periods.
Mitigate by: providing good quality, well-maintained accommodation at a fair market rent.

Risk: tenants causing damage to property.

Mitigate by: referencing tenants properly and insuring against malicious damage.

Risk: costs rising.
Mitigate by: testing your initial figures against a number of different cost base scenarios to make sure your investment still stacks up BEFORE you buy.

All of these factors can be tackled once you start researching your local property market, but the first risk you'll need to address is the risk that a lender takes in lending you mortgage finance.

Buy to let mortgages

Buy to let mortgages are different to residential mortgages in two main ways: the loan-to-value ratio is lower and is based primarily on the rental income potential of the property. I say 'primarily' because most (if not all) lenders will require you to have a personal income of at least £25,000 p/a before they'll consider you for a buy to let mortgage.

There are two steps you should take before approaching your financial advisor or mortgage broker:

1. Put together a personal financial statement: a document that lists all your assets, liabilities, income and expenditure, and that calculates your monthly cash flow and personal net worth. You can find templates if you do an online search.

2. Check your own credit score, via Experian or Equifax. As with any mortgage application, the lender will carry out a credit check on you, so make sure you're in the best possible position and if there is anything adversely affecting your score, contact the companies directly and see what you can do to sort the problem out – something like a missed payment is sometimes simply a misunderstanding that can be rectified. It also helps your score if you've lived at the same address for more than three years, have been employed for a number of years and are on the electoral roll.

Once a lender has established you're credit-worthy, how much they'll lend is usually calculated on the basis of the rental income (as verified by a surveyor) being at least 120%-130% of the monthly repayment amount. And, as things currently stand, you will probably be looking at a 75% LTV ratio.

Example, assuming a requirement of 125% x monthly repayment:

Property value   £200,000
Borrowing required at 75%   £150,000
Monthly mortgage repayment   £625   (£150,000 x 5% ÷ 12)
(at 5% mortgage interest rate, interest only)
Required rental valuation   £781 pcm (£625 x 125%)

Although the monthly rental income for an HMO is usually around £2,500+ pcm, most lenders won't accept a 'room rental' valuation, as they're always considering a worst-case scenario and will err on the side of safety – i.e. you only being able to rent the property as a single unit.

So you need to look for the kind of property that would not only make a good HMO but also rent well as a single unit let – otherwise you may have to be prepared to accept a lower LTV and put in more of your own capital, and that's not going to give you as good a return as if you gear highly.

A caveat to the above is that you might need a specialist HMO mortgage – which you almost certainly will with a licensable HMO – so you'll need to discuss it thoroughly with your broker or IFA. Lenders will look at whether you're buying something that's already classed as an HMO and will also need full disclosure on how you intend to rent the property, so you must make sure that you – and your financial representative – are declaring what's legally required.

One final thing you need to bear in mind is that lenders limit the number of buy to let mortgages an individual can have, so make sure that you thoroughly plan with your wealth manager, IFA and legal representative how to grow your portfolio legally and efficiently.

More creative ways of funding your investment...

I said at the start of the chapter that how you're able to finance your investments is dependent partly on finding the right people to work with and on your ability to build good relationships with those people. You'll only be able to embark on the more creative options if people trust you and you can prove to them that you know what you're doing, so there's no point in trying to approach investors for joint ventures (JVs) or put together a lease option or other 'creative purchase' proposition until you've got at least a couple of successful HMOs under your belt. In other words, there's no getting away from needing capital when you start out!

I've done many JVs and partnering with other people has allowed me to grow my portfolio far more quickly and easily than I would otherwise have been able to. And every one of those JVs is a true partnership – we share the risk and the reward equally – which is how you need to approach these deals. Finding the right people to partner with, whose investment goals you can satisfy and vice versa, isn't a quick process and it's not something you can really put a timescale on. People buy into people, so make sure the buzz surrounding you is that you're a) good at what you do and, b) ethical and decent in all your business dealings.

Always do what you've said you'll do,
when you've said you'll do it.

Tax & wealth planning

This is an incredibly important area of investment in general, and property tax is its own world. You may already have a tax advisor, but do they have experience of working specifically with buy to let investors? How you're taxed on your property investments will depend on a number of factors, such as how they are legally owned, how you take income from them and what other businesses and income you have, and everyone's situation is different.

As I've already said, you need to make sure that your HMO portfolio sits properly within the context of your existing financial/tax affairs and that property is, in fact, the right investment vehicle for you. So - if you haven't already - start looking into getting specialist, tailored advice now.

Checklist

Getting to grips with the financials

Have you done all these things?

☐ Put together a personal financial statement

☐ Discussed investment objectives with a financial advisor and assessed potential returns from property versus potential returns from other investments

☐ Sought out a specialist tax advisor and taken the time to really understand their advice

☐ Checked your credit score and taken steps to remedy any issues

☐ Fully considered key financial risk factors attached to HMO investments

☐ Investigated with your IFA the implications of needing an HMO-specific mortgage

☐ Put together an investment plan and clearly established how your investments will/can be financed

☐ Begun to think about what JVs might be appropriate for you in the future

Chapter 4

The legals

Buying, owning and letting investment property is very different to buying and owning your own home and, especially in the case of HMOs, there are numerous legal considerations you need to become familiar with.

One of the challenges of being an HMO investor is keeping on top of and up to date with all the legal requirements associated with your investment, so you'll need outside help and advice on an on-going basis. Some of this comes from engaging legal and financial professionals; some relies on you building relationships with local council departments and landlord associations; all of it demands that you, personally, understand the legal implications of every aspect of your property business.

Getting things right from the start will make life a lot easier and cheaper as you grow your portfolio. Too many investors 'dip their toe in the water' at the start by buying one HMO to see if they fancy it as an investment strategy. They take very little advice before they make their first investment, on the basis that they can 'sort it out later', if they decide to press on. What they don't realise is that there are on-going implications for the way some tax and legal matters are entered into and arranged at the outset.

Falling foul of your legal obligations can result in anything from a simple demand that you rectify a situation, to a criminal conviction, a hefty fine and prison time. In short, this is not an area you can afford to get wrong!

Although I'm not a qualified legal expert, I do have a great deal of hands-on experience as a 'consumer' in the field of HMO legals, so am going to highlight the key points I think you need to be aware of and regulations you need to comply with. I'm not going to go into a lot of detail because, a) I'm not a property lawyer, b) many of the precise legal requirements vary from council to council and, c) detail is what I pay experts for! You can spend an awful lot of time getting bogged down in research into specialist areas that others have spent years training for, so save yourself the time and effort and engage those experts to advise you.

The legal set-up and administration of your business

As I said in Chapter 1, it's important to speak to a wealth manager or independent financial advisor about your investment plans, so that they can look at property in the context of your other financial affairs. That will have an implication on the way you legally own your properties and structure your property business. Many buy to let investors own properties personally, then let and manage them through a Limited Company; some set up a new company, others use an existing one. For some people, having a company own a property portfolio is more suitable – everyone's situation is different and you need to work with financial and legal advisors to decide on the right set-up for you.

Having a Limited Company or Limited Liability Partnership brings its own associated legal requirements, including filing returns with Companies House and making declarations and filings with HMRC, and there can be heavy penalties for non-compliance. You will need to make sure your books are kept up to date and all legal and financial paperwork is filed properly.

Because HMO investing involves more certification, compliance and general paperwork than other types of property investment, I'd highly recommend you don't try to do it all yourself. I'll talk more about the team you should have around you later in the book, but three key members of that team should be:

1. a very good accountant who's a property tax expert
2. a legal representative with specific experience in buy to let investing
3. a bookkeeper experienced in buy to let – and preferably HMOs

You may be concerned with keeping costs down when you're starting out but, trust me, the cost of getting the right advice to make sure your business is correctly set up from the start is not a cost you should be cutting. Good professional advisors will end up saving you many times over what you pay them.

Conveyancing

Getting a good buy to let deal often relies on you being able to complete quickly, so your legal representative must be willing and able to move things along and look for solutions, not excuses! Look for a legal/ conveyancing firm that has experience specifically in the acquisition of properties for buy to let portfolios and try to make sure that the person dealing with your purchase is a buy to let investor themselves. They'll understand the things that are really important to you and know how to approach any problems that might come up.

As an HMO investor, it's more than likely you'll want – and usually need - to make alterations to the properties you buy, in order to make them fit for purpose. Extensions, movement or erection of walls and converting garages into bedrooms or living rooms are all very common, so whoever's carrying out your conveyancing needs to know these things are important to check in the property deeds – and/or lease, in the case of leasehold properties. New build deeds often prohibit the conversion of garages and leases often state that you can't alter any internal walls, and if a conveyancer fails to highlight any such clauses to you, you could end up with a property you can't let in the way you planned - and that could be disastrous for your investment strategy.

Similarly, they need to know to particularly check for any previous planning applications/issues and any upcoming changes in the law (such as the 'garden grabbing' legislation in 2010 that made it easier for local councils to refuse development requests) that might affect your plans for the property.

If you're buying with a spouse or business partner, you'll also need to decide whether to own the property as 'joint tenants' or 'tenants in common' for inheritance purposes (as joint tenants the property automatically passes to the other owner/s, whereas as tenants in common you can leave your share to any beneficiary in your will). A good legal representative should be able to help you with regard to your will and be willing and able to liaise with your wealth manager and mortgage broker to make sure you take ownership of the property in the right way, as quickly and efficiently as possible.

Planning

I don't think I'm over-exaggerating when I say that planning can be a minefield. You need to be aware that your investment is likely to be subject to certain planning laws and those laws vary from council to council – not only with regard to building works, but also change of use. Ignoring the issue of planning is not an option.

National legislation currently states that you don't need planning permission to change a property's use class from C3 (standard single household home) to C4 (HMO of up to 6 people), BUT local councils can adopt an Article 4 Direction requiring that you DO

www.nickfox.co.uk

63

apply for planning permission. The main issue with this is that the planning application process is likely to take longer than the conveyancing process, so you might end up completing on your purchase before a decision on whether to grant planning permission has been made!

You need to think very carefully about this, as entering into an investment that may turn out not to be fit for purpose could have serious financial implications for you. I've heard several horror stories about people who have bought properties without doing the necessary research – usually they've simply heard someone talk about the profitability of HMOs and have decided 'it doesn't sound that difficult to me…' – and they've ended up with a house in the wrong location that they can only let as a single unit, which doesn't cover their costs. They only have two choices: to let it out and keep subsidising the costs out of their own pockets, in the hope that the market will rise enough for them to sell and at least break even; or, to sell right away and take the financial hit.

The best you can do is talk to your local council planning department to find out what their policy is and approach your local landlords association to find out what other investors' experiences have been. There's also a lot of useful information on the Government's site: planningportal.gov.uk.

If you want your HMO to house more than six people, you will definitely need to gain planning permission, and I would always recommend you hire a local Chartered Town Planner to advise you and complete the application on your behalf. If you can build a good relationship with a planning expert, sometimes they're happy to give you a verbal idea as to whether a particular property would be likely to be granted planning permission (for change of use and also for any extensions or conversions you might want to carry out), although this would be in no way binding on their part.

Licensing

First things first: not all HMOs need to be licensed. National regulations (as per The Housing Act, 2004) state that HMOs only require a licence if:

- the property has three or more storeys
  AND
- it is occupied by five or more people, forming two or more households.

But local councils have the power to impose additional licensing in certain areas so, as with planning, you need to speak to them to find out their policy.

Licences are issued for five years and tend to cost between £100 and £200 a year, depending on where you live and how your local council calculates the charge – some charge per unit (i.e. per bedroom) and some per property. In my local area, the current charge is £885 for 5 years. I hear a lot of landlords talking about how expensive licensing is, but I don't think somewhere between

£8 and £17 a month is worth getting heated up over – especially when you consider the benefit of being able to tell your tenants that your HMO is registered with the council and meets approved living and health & safety standards.

If your property is subject to licensing, your local authority will check it to make sure there's enough space for all the tenants and that it's being managed properly. You'll also need to comply with gas and electrical safety, health & safety and fire safety requirements – which, no surprise, tend to vary from council to council!

Building regulations (an extension of Planning)

Another area where you need to make sure you're compliant. People sometimes make the mistake of thinking that if they're not actually 'building' anything – i.e. extending or converting lofts etc. – then building regulations don't concern them. Wrong.

The main thing to know here is that if you're undertaking *any* work to the property, you must speak to the council about their building regulations policy BEFORE you start works, otherwise you can get in a mess, with regard to both their assessment and potentially having to redo work.

As well as having to comply with general building regulations, your HMO may need soundproofing. The planning department can advise you of this – usually it's only an issue with licensable HMOs – but it's not something you want to come as a surprise, because it can cost tens of thousands to soundproof a whole house.

Health & Safety

If your HMO is licensable, then the council will advise you of everything you need to do health and safety-wise to make sure your licence is granted. But even if you don't need one, it's a really good idea – certainly on the first one or two properties you buy – to have someone from the housing department visit (Housing Standards Officer, or similar) to check you're doing things properly.

As a landlord, you have a legal duty of care to your tenants and must carry out a fire safety risk assessment, to show that you've identified and considered all potential risks and taken steps to mitigate them. You could do this yourself, but for around £200 a qualified Fire Risk Assessor will carry out the assessment for you and not only make sure you're doing everything legally required (such as ensuring your furnishings and furniture comply with fire regulations), but also make recommendations for additional sensible steps to take – for example, installing smoke detectors in all rooms (heat sensors in the kitchen) and fitting fire doors to all bedrooms and kitchens.

As far as how many of the 'additional recommendations' you should implement is concerned, a good rule of thumb is: are you satisfied that if anything happened to one of your tenants and you ended up in court, you could honestly say – and prove - you'd taken all reasonable steps to ensure their safety? That's why instructing a professional to carry out the risk assessment and going over and above the basic legal requirements are both advisable…I like to sleep at night!

Certification required

HMOs, where tenants are sharing kitchens and bathrooms, don't currently legally need a valid Energy Performance Certificate (EPC), but I'm sure that will change in the future and so suggest you make one available to your tenants anyway.

What you absolutely DO need is:

1. An annual gas safety check, carried out by a Gas Safe registered engineer, and that record must be made available to the tenants (and copied to the local council if the property is licensed).
2. An Electrical Installation Condition Report certificate. All fixed electrical installations must be inspected and tested by a qualified electrician at least every five years and the local authority can require the certificate to be produced in 7 days – for any HMO, not just a licensed one.

As you've probably gathered, because so much of the legislation around HMOs is defined by local councils, it's absolutely imperative you speak to the various departments – and don't presume they speak to each other! – to find out their overall attitude to HMOs and exactly where you stand with regard to:

- Planning
- Licensing
- Building regulations (including soundproofing)

- Electrical safety certification
- Fire safety (and speak to your local Fire Safety or Community Safety Officer)

Your local landlords association should also be a great source of information - I've found most other landlords are only too happy to share their experiences and steer you in the right direction.

The legal agreement between you and your house sharers

The document you should be using to form the legal contract between you and your tenants is an Assured Shorthold Tenancy Agreement (AST). In student properties, where it's usually a group of friends moving in together, it's common for there to be just one AST, which makes all the tenants jointly and severally liable for the total rent. But with HMOs for working adults, who usually don't know each other and don't want to assume responsibility for the rent in this way, landlords tend to issue separate ASTs for each room.

The key thing is that you understand and comply with your rights and responsibilities as a landlord. In simple terms, you are obliged to:
- provide suitable, secure accommodation
- properly maintain all fixtures, fittings and furnishings you've provided, in addition to the fabric of the property itself
- ensure the health and safety of your tenants

- allow your tenants peaceful occupation of the property
- give adequate written notice to terminate the agreement

You can buy an AST 'off the shelf', from a stationers or online, but most landlords tend to want to customise it. DON'T simply do this yourself! You could end up in a legal mess if any additional clauses were to be challenged, so always use a legal letting specialist to ensure that, a) the agreement is appropriate for letting to a tenant of an HMO and, b) all terms are legally enforceable. It's worth spending a few hundred pounds getting the contract right in the beginning, because you're going to be issuing a lot of them and need to be confident that your adapted AST will stand up in court.

Checklist

The legals

Have you done all these things?

Legal advice

☐ Spoken to a wealth advisor, property tax expert and legal representative with specific experience in buy to let investing

☐ Researched local legal firms to find a good buy to let expert

Planning

☐ Spoken to local council planning department to find out local policy:

☐ Is planning permission required for change of use?

☐ What is the general policy with regard to development?

☐ Spoken to local landlords association about planning regulations and recent decisions

☐ Checked on www.planningportal.gov.uk/buildingregulations

Licensing

☐ Looked at www.gov.uk/house-in-multiple-occupation-licence

☐ Spoken to local council about its HMO licensing policy

☐ Spoken to local landlords association about specific local requirements

Health & Safety
☐ Spoken to local council & landlords association
☐ Looked at www.firesafe.org.uk/houses-in-multiple-occupation/
☐ Obtained a Fire Risk Assessment form (freely available online)

Tenancy agreement
☐ Read through a standard AST and understood rights and responsibilities
☐ Spoken to a legal lettings specialist

PART TWO:

SECURING YOUR

INVESTMENT AND

PREPARING TO LET

Chapter 5

Become your own local expert

As you're probably gathering, there aren't any short cuts to becoming a successful HMO investor – either financially or in terms of time and effort! You'll get the best results from buying a property with built-in equity that's in high demand – i.e. the right property, in the right location, at the right price – and doing that requires expertise.

While you can 'outsource' legal, financial, trades and management expertise, the best person to source property on an on-going basis is you. You can tap into the knowledge and services of local estate and letting agents who know the area well, but they're highly unlikely to be experts in sourcing HMOs, so you're going to have to be able to quickly assess yourself what's going to work and what isn't.

Don't make the mistake of chasing after deals around the country, or let yourself be persuaded by investment companies and people selling leads that they've discovered the 'new hot spot' and can let you share in the good fortune of 'an incredible deal – but hurry, or you'll miss out...' Almost every town and city in the UK has a shortage of multi-let accommodation and you can always find some kind of good deal locally, provided you know where and how to look, and how to negotiate.

Why doing it yourself is better than buying leads

Whoever's selling leads will tell you how well they know the area and how great their contacts are. They'll say they're either not in a position to buy the properties themselves or aren't interested in expanding their own portfolio any further, so are looking to gain some financial reward in another way: the fee they charge you for benefiting from their expertise.

The main issue with buying leads where you simply pay a fee is that the 'expert' selling to you has no on-going interest in the property you buy. They get their fee whether or not you ultimately make money from the property, and when you're looking at investing as much capital as you are in an HMO, that's an awful lot of faith to be putting in someone else. I've come across far too many people who've bought leads that have turned out to be bad investments – at best, they just about break even; at worst, they're left with a property that's not worth what they paid for it and which nobody wants to rent at anything like a reasonable market rate. Yes, you can – and should – do your own research on any property you're considering buying, to satisfy yourself that it's a good deal and meets your objectives, but then what are you paying the sourcer for?

Look at how much they want to charge and work out how much of your own time that could buy – time you could spend getting to know your area really well – and you'll see that working on becoming your own local expert is a far better long-term investment.

Why invest locally?

The question is, really, why not? If you happen to live in an area that doesn't have sufficient demand for HMOs (often the case with rural locations), you might need to look as far as an hour away, maybe more. But, as a rule, you will be able to find solid investment properties within easy striking distance – 15 to 30 minutes - of your home.

Benefits of basing your portfolio locally:

1. **You can focus your efforts.** You can't possibly become an expert in all the various micro-markets in the UK, so why not focus on a place you already know something about? By concentrating on just one area, you give yourself the best chance of success in that area.

2. **You can be where you need to be quickly.** Good deals often need acting on right away so there's a real advantage in being able to look at a property as soon as you hear about it and meet with vendors and agents. Even if you have someone else fully managing your portfolio, there will be times you'll want or need to visit your properties or deal in person with some issue, which is a lot easier – saving you time and expense - when you're close-by.

3. **It'll be easier to build good relationships.** You'll

be on hand to liaise regularly with estate and letting agents, attend local property and networking events and can tap into existing contacts to find good tradespeople and suppliers Also, there's often a natural resistance to property investors from homeowners, but if you're a local yourself, you may find it easier to overcome that and also to negotiate with vendors.

4. **You can build your profile locally.** Become known for doing what you say you'll do and for running an ethical, reputable business. I have ***never*** shaken hands on a deal and then backed out, even when it's turned out not to be quite as good as I first believed. Your reputation is everything, so make sure people want to do business with you and talk about you for the right reasons. Get involved with local events and give back to your community, whether it's offering your time and expertise for free or helping financially, such as sponsoring a local sports team. Just make sure you do it for the right reasons and choose things that mean something to you – I'm talking about good PR, not shameless self-promotion!

"It takes many good deeds to build a good reputation and only one bad deed to lose it."
Benjamin Franklyn

And as your business and reputation grows, you'll find that other successful people will gravitate towards you and more and more opportunities will come your way – and not just in the property sphere. Through building my HMO portfolio I've been invited to lots of different business and social events and have now become a huge fan of motor racing and horseracing! I've built friendships with people I've met at those events and have already partnered with several of them on different projects.

The expertise you'll need to gain

You need to immerse yourself in the property market so that you know exactly which properties, in which streets, at what price, will make good HMOs. And to make sure they're a good investment not only today but also into the future, you need to understand market trends and be able to spot local economic indicators.

The ability to value a property

Valuing a property is not an exact science – ultimately you can say that a property is only worth what someone will pay for it on a given day – but you need to get to the point where you have an instinctive feel for a fair price. You can only do that by building a bank of knowledge about what's recently been sold and looking at market trends, then putting that knowledge together with the current supply and demand situation: how much of what you're looking for is currently on the market and how many people are competing for that type of property?

You can find sold property prices online – **rightmove.co.uk** and **landregistry.gov.uk** are two of the best sources – but it's also worth spending time talking to estate agents. They'll be able to speak about specific areas with more knowledge, give you details of potential HMOs that have recently sold, and it's also a good way of testing which agents might be the best ones to try and work with going forward. You'll quickly see the ones that understand buy to let and are interested in building longer-term relationships with investors/landlords.

A couple of good online tools for seeing what's currently happening to prices in your local area are:

- **propertysnake.co.uk**, where you can put in a postcode and it will show you how long a property's been listed online and when and by how much each property was reduced in price
- **the Property-Bee toolbar** for Firefox, which will bring up all changes to the price and details made since the property was listed, for any property you look at on Rightmove and PrimeLocation, as well as a few other sites.

Using these tools, together with the information you get from agents, and your own additional research, should give you a very good idea of values.

Buying at the right price is so important for an investor. When it's your own home, you're often prepared to pay a little more than you really wanted to because of the emotional investment, but this is strictly business, so make sure you have 'number-crunched' thoroughly and are as sure as you can be that the property will not only deliver the cash flow you need, but also be a good long-term investment. Look at how average house prices in the region have performed over the past 20 years and then compare how the kind of properties you've identified as good potential HMOs have performed against that average. You should aim to buy property that has consistently outperformed - or, at the very least, kept up with – the local average, because that's a very good indicator that it will continue to do the same.

Recognising economic drivers

These are key to supply and demand in an area, affecting both the capital value of your investment and on-going income potential. HMOs are most successful in areas where there are good transport links, decent local amenities, employment opportunities and a shortage of quality accommodation.

A lot of people simply look at what's going on in the area at the moment and whether it's 'regenerating', and that's a fair indication that there may be good current demand. But where's the investment coming from and what's the future plan? Wine bars and restaurants come and go; you need to know what the local plans are for the next 5-20 years, because you're in this business for the long term. You have to be as certain as you can that the demand for rooms isn't going to suddenly fall because either businesses are closing down in the area or a whole load of new multi-let accommodation has suddenly been granted planning permission.

Information about future plans for the area is freely available from your local council, but you can usually get more in-depth information from speaking to local businesspeople, other investors, good estate agents and surveyors who have lived and worked in the area for a while. And revisit this research every six months or so to make sure you're always aware of what's coming up and can adjust your investment (by changing how you let and who to, or selling and reinvesting in another property), if necessary.

The local council's attitude to HMOs

Given that pretty much every council will have a slightly different policy and attitude towards HMOs, you need to become an expert in yours. You must know exactly where their boundaries fall, because neighbouring councils can have different regulations, for example, one might have adopted the Article 4 Direction requiring you to seek planning permission for any HMO, while the other might be happy for up to 6 people to share a house without planning. A common issue is parking: some councils will only permit an HMO if there is a certain amount of off-road parking with the property; others don't mind whether there is or not. Another consideration is how 'C3' they view an area, i.e. are there certain pockets that are considered 'family home-friendly', where the council would refuse permission for a property to be rented out as an HMO? Depending on a council's attitude (and taking into account all your other research), you may decide not to invest in a certain ward if there are too many requirements and restrictions.

Tenant preferences

Different types of tenants often have certain areas - even particular streets - that they like to live in, so you need to research where the kind of people you want to rent to are requesting rooms. Sites such as **spareroom.co.uk** and **uk.easyroommate.com** have 'wanted' adverts and you can usually see their employment status. Letting agents, even though they might not rent rooms out themselves, often know the particularly popular and not so popular areas. Working adults, for example, tend not to like living in a particularly student-oriented area and want somewhere they can park, so narrower streets without off-road parking, within walking distance of a university won't be suitable.

And find out what they're looking for, in particular. All house sharers prefer refurbished properties with decent kitchens and bathrooms and many expect wireless broadband, but what else does your target market expect – and are they happy to pay more for it? Is a cleaner expected, or satellite TV? You want to provide whatever there is a demand for, and a shortage of.

Rental values

While average property prices tend to peak and trough, rents are usually fairly consistent, so their performance over time isn't so relevant. What you need to focus on is how much tenants are prepared to pay for what level of accommodation. HMOs vary wildly in quality, so the average room rent for your area might actually be significantly lower than you could charge for what you're offering. Where I invest, double rooms vary between £350 and £500 a month.

As with the above, look online at what people are prepared to pay for an all-inclusive room rent – SpareRoom puts out a monthly index of room rental prices, which you can access from the website for free - and then go and look at some of your competitors' properties. Get to know exactly what standard you need to provide so that you can charge the highest reasonable rent and still keep the property full.

You must also make sure you know the rental values for letting a property like yours as a single unit because, as I mentioned in Chapter 3, lenders may be basing their mortgage calculations on that single let value. An area might stack up well on purchase price and on-going cash flow potential, but if it's an area that tends to attract low-income families, the monthly rental value for letting the property as a family home might be too low to make the purchase worthwhile, because of the amount of deposit you'd have to put in. Talk to local letting agents about your plans and ask their professional advice on which areas might be best to consider, then back it up with your own online research.

All the elements above combine to give you a detailed picture of the local HMO market. As you build your knowledge of values and analyse them together with costs and income to calculate potential returns, you'll start to see which areas/streets are most viable, with the right balance between accommodation potential, affordability, demand and capital growth potential.

There is no secret to success; it is the result of preparation, hard work and sheer determination.

Checklist

Becoming your own local expert

Have you done all these things?

Property prices and trends

- ☐ Researched sold price data on rightmove.co.uk and landregistry.gov.uk
- ☐ Looked at how 'for sale' prices are currently shifting, via propertysnake.co.uk and Property-Bee
- ☐ Compared the performance of 'HMO type' properties with the market average over the last 20 years
- ☐ Spoken to local agents about the current local market and trends

HMO-specific research

- ☐ Established local council's attitude to HMOs
- ☐ Checked the areas in which planning and licensing are needed
- ☐ Researched rental values for letting both rooms and the property as a single unit
- ☐ Looked at the rental index data on spareroom.co.uk/rentalindex
- ☐ Researched tenant demand: exactly what do they want, and where?
- ☐ Been to visit existing HMOs for competitor research
- ☐ Tested purchase and rental figures on an HMO viability spreadsheet

Chapter 6

Your team

Once you've researched your local HMO market thoroughly, you should have a level of expertise that very few other people will have. Most of the professionals you'll deal with as you source, buy, refurbish, let and manage your portfolio won't know as much as you do about the market as a whole – and that puts you in a great position for being able to ask the right questions and pick the best people to work with.

There are some very good reasons why you should surround yourself with advisors, suppliers and associates:

1. You can't be an expert in everything, so the very best thing you can do for your business is tap into the knowledge, skills and resources of the people who *are* experts in their own specific area of property investment.
2. By outsourcing as much as possible, you're freeing up your own time. And, as you become better at finding and negotiating great deals and running your business, your time will be worth many times more than the cost of paying someone else to do various jobs.

3. Property can be a lonely business if you do most of the work yourself – you'll find it much more enjoyable with a good team and network around you.

I use the services of more than 20 different people on a regular basis. They're all very good at what they do, which enables me to acquire properties efficiently and for the business to run with minimal daily input from me. I think of these people as my 'team':

*   Wealth manager
*   Buy to let specialist property lawyers
*   Independent mortgage broker
*   Accountant
*   Bookkeeper
*   Estate agents
*   PA
*   Property manager
*   Lettings negotiators
*   Project manager for refurbishments
*   Maintenance team and specialist contractors

Since I began investing, there have been some changes to my team, and you may find you don't get the perfect people first time around. But I've worked with all my current advisors, suppliers and employees for a number of years now and am happy that it's a very strong line-up.

Your key players

**All professionals giving you financial advice MUST be properly qualified and regulated by the Financial Services Authority (FSA) and anyone giving you legal advice should be suitably qualified and regulated by The Law Society and the Solicitors Regulation Authority (SRA) (or the Council of Licensed Conveyancers (CLC)).

Wealth Manager

As I've already said, property investment needs to fit properly alongside your other financial interests. Whether you choose to engage a wealth management firm or take advantage of your bank's wealth management service, try to work with someone who either invests in property themselves or already has a number of property investor clients. It'll short-cut your discussions and they're likely to have researched the subject very well indeed.

Take your investment objectives and personal financial statement along to your meeting, so that the wealth manager can get a clear picture of your current situation and where you want to get to. They can then help you decide the best way to structure your investments.

Importantly, they can also help you with inheritance planning. Too many people invest in property so they have something to leave to their children, without realising that it can be one of the least tax-efficient ways to pass on money. You'll need to amend your will and may need to set up Trusts – it's a complex area, and demands specialist advice.

As well as being FSA regulated, ideally they will also have the CISI Masters in Wealth Management (MCSI after their name).

Property tax specialist / accountant

Wealth management firms are usually able to give you tax advice and handle your accounts, but you must make sure that you've had a proper discussion with someone who is a property tax expert. As I said earlier in the book, your investment plans will impact your current tax situation - and vice versa, - and a specialist will be able to advise you how to set up and run your HMO business in the most tax-efficient way.

Mortgage broker / IFA

Your mortgage broker can make or break a deal. You're looking for someone who understands exactly what you're aiming for and appreciates that things often need to happen quickly. Make sure they're independent (i.e. can access all mortgage products in the market) and have worked in buy to let for a number of years, as they're likely to have established relationships with buy to let and HMO specialist lenders.

I'd never attempt to find a mortgage myself by going direct to different lenders, for three key reasons:

1. It can be incredibly time-consuming and I'm not a mortgage expert.

2. Good brokers usually have access to mortgage products that aren't publicised – you only know they're there if you ask about them, and if you don't know they're there…!

3. As an individual, trying to contact lenders to progress an application can be an incredibly frustrating experience and you're unlikely to have any luck moving it along quickly. An effective broker will be able to access the right people and push your application through.

Never underestimate the value a good broker can add to your business. Being well-financed will mean you'll not only be able to act quickly on deals, but also get better deals and be more profitable.

Any person acting as a broker or making recommendations for your mortgage finance must have one or more of these qualifications: Certificate in Mortgage Advice (Cert MA); Certificate in Mortgage Advice and Practice (CeMAP) from the ifa School of Finance; Mortgage Advice and Practice Certificate (MAPC) from the CIB in Scotland.

Specialist property lawyer

Ideally, they should be buy to let specialists and have experience of dealing with HMO investors. As with your broker, your legal representative can make the difference between a smooth and speedy transaction and a complete nightmare! You can instruct either a solicitor or a licensed conveyancer – both are qualified to handle property transactions – but one of the benefits of engaging a solicitor is that you can choose a firm that also has solicitors specialising in other areas of law. That means your legal representative can tap into the knowledge of colleagues for advice on things like tax planning, wills, litigation, etc. and you may be able to keep all your legal affairs under one roof.

Some firms have specific case-progression departments; some solicitors/conveyancers will progress things themselves. Both have pros and cons - the important thing for you to establish is:

1. Are they happy to work to a timescale established at the start (unforeseen circumstances aside)?
2. Will they update you regularly?
3. Will you be able to easily speak to the person directly dealing with your transaction?

You also need to make sure that whoever you choose is happy to liaise and work closely with your broker/IFA and wealth manager to keep your business on track with your objectives.

I realise I'm painting a picture of perfection here, but these legal representatives do exist! Take personal recommendations from other investors and meet in person with all those on your 'shortlist'. Homebuyers usually engage solicitors over the phone, or online, but when it's someone who's going to be so crucial to the success of your business over a number of years, you need to make sure there's a good personal relationship and understanding from the start.

The other person who can really help you stay on the right side of the law is a local planning expert. Planning regulations have a tendency to change rather quietly, so if you can build a relationship with a Chartered Town Planner, they can guide you and help you minimize the risk of falling foul of regulations.

Estate agents

You might be lucky enough to have local estate agents who already understand about investing in HMOs, but it's more likely that you'll have to 'train' them. Avoid agents who want to take your contact details before they've even asked what you're looking for – focus on the ones who actually want to have a conversation with you. You also want someone who knows the area and market well, so try to deal with senior negotiators or the branch manager, as they're more likely to be able to have a productive discussion.

Independent agents are usually owned and/or managed by people who have lived and worked in the area for quite some time. They're often on local boards and well-connected, so can be a very useful source of information about planning, upcoming developments, people who might be interested in JVs, etc.

Talk to the agents about your plans, show them you have your finances and legal representation in place, then view a few properties and explain exactly what's right and wrong, so they build up a picture of your ideal HMO. Contact and feedback are key; always do what you say you'll do, view properties they recommend right away and keep them posted on what stage you're at in any transactions so they don't need to 'chase' you.

You want to get to a position where you have three or four agents that understand exactly what you're looking for, know you'll act quickly and make sensible offers, so will call you as soon as they see a property that might be suitable. The quicker a sale can be agreed and completed, the sooner the agents get their money – you're an agent's dream! – so don't give them any reason not to want to have you at the top of their buyer list.

Agents MUST be members of The Property Ombudsman. Ideally, deal with agents who are Fellows of the National Association of Estate Agents (FNAEA) and/or the Royal Institution of Chartered Surveyors (FRICS).

Reliable contractors

Reliable contractors are worth their weight in gold – and then some. You need a team for your refurbishment projects and then a team that can handle on-going maintenance. While you'll probably be able to use many of the same people, some contractors prefer to only handle larger projects and some only smaller ones, which is often the case with electricians and plumbers. The most important thing is that you hire the right people for each job.

Refurbishment core team:
- Builder (ideally who can also project manage – otherwise

you may need someone else to manage it), preferably a member of the Federation of Master Builders

- Plasterer
- Painter/decorator
- Glazier, FENSA regulated
- Locksmith, ideally from the Master Locksmiths Association
- Carpet fitter
- Plumber, Gas Safe registered
- Electrician, 'Part P' registered
- Cleaner

You may be tempted to project manage the refurbishment yourself, but I'd highly recommend you employ someone else to do it. The refurb contractors need to be able to work together – if they all have their own agendas, you can find projects stall or take longer than necessary because they're all blaming each other for not being able to get on to the next stage. A project manager (often a builder) will have a regular team that he knows will work efficiently together and you pay him to make sure everything stays on track. It also means you only have one person to liaise with.

Maintenance core team:
- General handyman
- Plumber, Gas Safe registered
- Electrician, 'Part P' registered (for general maintenance and safety checks)
- Portable Appliance Tester

- Gardener (the handyman may do this for you)
- Emergency locksmith, ideally from the Master Locksmiths Association
- Cleaner

You'll need to call on most of these people at short notice, so do everything you can to make sure they respond to you quickly. A very good way of ensuring they do is to make sure you pay them quickly when they invoice. Most – if not all – of these people will be self-employed and/or running small businesses and really can't afford to wait several weeks for payment, so will greatly appreciate you settling their bills right away.

The cost of your team

Cost is something that always comes up when I speak to investors who are just starting out and it's a significant concern for those who only have the funds to finance one property initially. They're worried that they're going to end up spending too high a proportion of their money on good advice, particularly with financial and legal professionals, and that's entirely understandable, but legal and financial advice isn't something you should scrimp on.

It's hard to say how much is 'reasonable' for someone to charge you for advice; what I'd say is that you should most definitely feel you're getting value for money. In your initial preparation and research, you should have worked out how much your own time is worth, looked at the risks and associated potential costs of getting things wrong, and therefore be able to work out whether the costs you're being quoted for mitigating those risks and greatly reducing the chance of succumbing to the potential pitfalls of investing are fair.

"Where do I find good contractors?"

What people are usually asking with that question, is whether I can give them a list of reliable people to use! As with so much of this business, you get the best results if you do your own homework, which means networking locally with other landlords and asking friends to recommend contractors they've used. You can also look on websites such as RatedPeople.com and mybuilder.com, where tradespeople have been rated on their work.

Two important things to check are: 1) that any contractor you use has their own insurance and, 2) whether they have some formal accreditation or membership of a relevant industry body, so a good place to start is **trustmark.org.uk**, which has a database of tradespeople that operate to government-endorsed standards. If someone you're considering isn't listed on there, that doesn't mean you shouldn't use them, but do check their credentials thoroughly to make sure they're properly qualified for the job you need them to do, and insured against any damage they might cause.

And when you speak to contractors about what you need them to do, be honest and clear about your future plans. You want to try from the start to use people who will be willing and able to work for you as your portfolio grows.

Building good relationships with all the people on your team is vital to your success. You're going be dealing with them on a fairly regular basis – some more often than others – so it's important that they're not only very good at what they do and understand your business, but that you actually get on with them. When you like the people you do business with, and they like you, things get done more efficiently and everyone wins.

> *"Pretend that every single person you meet has a sign around his or her neck that says, 'Make me feel important'. Not only will you succeed in sales, you will succeed in life."*
> **Mary Kay Ash, Entrepreneur**

As well as my professional team, I also get a lot of good ideas and advice from other investors and businesspeople that I choose to spend time with. When I started out, I went to every 'property meet' and seminar I could find, but I honestly didn't find them very helpful, mainly because they weren't focused enough on what I wanted to do and there were too many people simply trying to sell to me. That's not to say you might not get something from going along to some, but I'd suggest you're selective.

Visit one or two of the larger national property investment and landlord shows/exhibitions and listen to as many relevant seminars as you can. If what they say makes sense to you, talk to the speakers afterwards and ask them their opinion on which meets and events are worth attending. And talk to other visitors – you'll find that most people can't wait to discuss their portfolio! Make sure you've already done a lot of your objective planning and market research before you go, so you'll really be able to focus on the people you think it might be worth meeting with again.

Summary

Putting together and changing your team...

You need to have some of your team in place before you start looking for properties and others you can pick up along the way. I would certainly recommend that you don't take any investment action without having consulted the key financial and legal professionals:

- ☐ A wealth adviser/manager
- ☐ An independent financial adviser (IFA)
- ☐ A property tax specialist
- ☐ A buy to let specialist mortgage broker (your IFA may fulfil this role)
- ☐ An experienced buy to let solicitor or licensed conveyancer

As you start searching for properties, you will identify:
- ☐ Estate & letting agents
- ☐ A project manager
- ☐ Renovation/refurbishment tradespeople
- ☐ Maintenance contractors

And, as your portfolio grows, you will need to recruit:
- ☐ A bookkeeper and accountant (your tax adviser may take care of this for you)
- ☐ A property manager
- ☐ A PA/administrator

Your team will, undoubtedly, change over time. Some will move jobs or retire, and you'll probably find that others are just not a good fit for you and your business. And, while it's certainly inconvenient to have to source new professional specialists and contractors, it's something that simply comes with the turf, so make sure you're always aware of good local people that may be able to help you in the future.

Chapter 7

Researching properties

If you've already done everything I've outlined so far, you'll be in a very good position to research properties. Just to recap, by this point you should be able to tick off the following:

- Established financial and lifestyle objectives and created some kind of visual reminders of these
- Put together a personal financial statement
- Looked into what's involved in running a small business
- Researched and considered the risks and downsides of investing in HMOs
- Met with a wealth manager (or at the very least an IFA) and put in place an investment plan
- Dealt with business set-up, inheritance issues and your will
- Established available financing options with a mortgage broker/IFA
- Engaged (or at least identified) a suitable legal representative
- Done some initial local area research into supply and demand and sales and rental values
- Investigated good local contractors

The first thing you have to be clear on is who's going to rent your rooms and what they're looking for, because demand is the driver for your business. You can then start looking at the best way to satisfy that demand in a way that meets your financial objectives.

Your target market

I'd say that working adults between the ages of 20 and 35 will make up the vast majority of your tenants and they'll have all kinds of different requirements, depending on their job and personal situations. There might be a shortage of rooms in certain specific locations, for example, for NHS staff near a hospital or for commuting professionals close to a station, but, as a general rule, you need to cast your net wide and make sure your property appeals to as many people as possible.

General wants and needs of people renting rooms:
- A good-sized double room
- Reliable shower/bath
- Plenty of space in the kitchen
- On a bus / train / tram / tube route
- Easy walking distance to shops
- Parking
- Warmth!
- Broadband
- *In certain, usually high-value areas in and around London, working professionals will expect an en-suite*

Some of the things we tend to be very concerned about when we're looking for a home to buy - such as a garden and sitting room – simply aren't that important when you're talking about an HMO. Fundamentally, people want a good private space and decent washing and cooking facilities; how well you satisfy the other requirements will make the difference between you letting your rooms more quickly than your competitors and being able to charge the top rents in the area. See Chapter 9 for more details.

Online research

These days you can find a huge amount of very up-to-date information, about prices, room-seekers and properties, quickly and easily online. You will need to talk to agents to get some more specific local information, but start with the internet so that you're well-prepared for your discussions in person and can get used to analysing figures. The more online research you do, the better a feel you'll get for which properties in which areas would be worth viewing.

Tenant demand/s

You need to research what the demand *is* and what the demand is *for*. The top three sites I'd suggest you use are: spareroom.co.uk, uk.easyroommate.com and gumtree.com. Go to the 'rooms wanted' section, put in your town or city name and see how many people are looking for rooms. Then do the same search for rooms advertised, and if there are at least twice as many 'wanted' adverts as there are rooms available, it's worth taking your research further.

Go back to the 'rooms wanted' section and see which specific areas the people who are prepared to pay most want to live in. Again, put that area name or postcode into the 'rooms available' search and look at the supply/demand ratio. Once you've identified the areas where demand is outstripping supply by at least 100%, you can start to focus in on exactly what people are looking for, in terms of room size, communal facilities, parking/bike storage and broadband/ satellite TV, so you can start making a list of refurbishment requirements and associated budget.

Remember to use this research alongside your general area research for future demand. For instance, an area might have quite an average supply/demand balance at the moment, but if inward investment has already been allocated for transport or facilities, or businesses have confirmed plans to move into the area, they're strong indicators that buying into the area now could actually be a very good investment.

Property values

Rightmove.co.uk and landregistry.gov.uk are two of the most useful sites for checking past and current property values. You can search for properties by postcode and make comparisons over time, even breaking it down into types of housing stock (detached houses, semi-detached houses, flats, etc.). The thing you won't usually be able to see is the condition of each property, but if you look at enough data, you should be able to get a pretty good idea of how much each type of property in each area is worth.

I'd suggest that you base most of your initial research on properties - in areas of high room rental demand - that could provide a minimum of:

- 5 double bedrooms and one single
- Two bathrooms (one of which could be a shower room)
- A large kitchen/dining room
  or
- Good-sized kitchen and a separate living room

Those are the basics of a fairly average HMO, which usually comes from reconfiguring/converting/extending a property that's currently being used as a family home. That might be something that:

- Already has all the required rooms if you simply reconfigure a current sitting room and dining room as bedrooms
- Offers the potential for conversion of a garage or conservatory into a bedroom or living area
- Has one or two large rooms that could be split into two – or more rooms

…hopefully you get the idea. Most of the properties that offer enough space will be detached or semi-detached houses with three or four bedrooms, so start searching with those criteria.

You can easily spend several days looking at prices and comparing areas in terms of how much space you get for your money, which areas are holding their values well, and which have suffered badly during the recession. Don't get too bogged down – all you need is to identify a reasonably accurate price range that you can use to work the investment viability numbers, and an idea of which areas are likely to hold their capital values.

While you're looking at the property prices, also try to note how long properties have been on the market and by how much the original asking price has been reduced. As mentioned in Chapter 5, Propertysnake.co.uk tracks properties for sale nationwide and details when and by how much the property has been reduced, and the Property-Bee toolbar for Firefox gives much the same information. This will help you build up an idea of the demand for each kind of property, as well as a realistic value, and also support your reasoning for future offers.

(And don't forget to check the rental values for letting this kind of property as a single unit, as that figure may be used by your lender in calculating your mortgage amount.)

Narrowing it down…

You'll need to look at a **lot** of property details – probably over 100 - in order to end up with a shortlist of ten or so that are worth viewing. Most online details include a floor plan, which makes your life a lot easier, as you can quickly see whether the layout is going to work for you.

Once you find a potentially suitable property that's in the right location, at the right sort of value, you can really start number-crunching, using different purchase price scenarios, maximum and minimum expected rental prices and approximate refurbishment costs. Your spreadsheet should be set up with formulae to auto-calculate yield, ROI and profit so that you can easily compare the KPIs for each property. (This can and will be refined if you actually decide to proceed to offer, but for now you just need to know that it's financially worth pursuing.)

Armed with the printed details of the properties on your shortlist, you can now leave the house!

Doing the legwork

Before you go and see any of the selling agents, have a drive past the properties, to get an impression of the location. Some things to consider:

- If there are loads of 'room to rent' signs around, you may not have done your research properly
- If there are lots of 'for sale' boards, that's a sign supply is exceeding demand and you may be able to get a good deal on the price
- Look at the general state of the neighbourhood – does it appear relatively safe and reasonably well maintained?
- What's the parking situation?
- Are there any off-putting things not mentioned on the

online details, such as derelict buildings or electrical substations?

And do you like the look of the property? Although you're not going to be living in it yourself, you may need or want to sell at some point and you're certainly looking for something that will keep up with or exceed average capital values for the area. I always trust my gut when I look at a property and if I don't really like the look of it, regardless of what the figures say, I won't buy it.

Once you're happy with your drive-bys, book viewings. If you've already met with the agents when you were doing your initial area/agent research, you can make telephone appointments, but if you haven't, make sure you go into the branch, introduce yourself and explain what you're doing. Ask the agents for their opinions on the properties you've shortlisted – including ones that are on with other agents - and don't forget to check whether they have any new instructions that might be suitable, even if they haven't yet got hard-copy details. You need to build an open, trusting relationship with the people who will probably be your main source of new acquisitions.

Viewing properties

When you're viewing a potential HMO for the first time, try to simply think of it as a box and don't get distracted by how it looks at the moment. Any wall that's not supporting can be removed; stud walls can be put up; garages and conservatories can be converted; bathrooms and kitchens can be refitted and/or new ones created.

What you really need to look out for are the things that can add significant expense to a refurbishment project and/or that may make the property unsuitable, such as:

- Can all prospective bedrooms be easily accessed from communal areas?
- Are there any wall cracks wider than a 10p coin? That often indicates significant movement, possibly subsidence.
- Which side/end of the house is the plumbing currently on? Extending an existing plumbing system or installing a completely new one can be major works.
- Does the roof look in reasonable condition and is the chimney stack straight?
- Are many of the windows single-glazed?
- Is there a connection to a telephone exchange?

Have a good look round outside, checking for anything you couldn't see when you did your drive-by and look at any potential for building or extension – even if you're not planning anything at the moment, you might want to in the future.

A bit of advice for when you're looking at all this on your first visit is not to say too much about your plans to the vendor. Most of the properties you'll be looking at will be someone's home that they've loved and raised a family in, and the last thing they want to hear is that you're planning on ripping out walls and fixtures, painting over all their lovely décor and installing fire doors. Some vendors can get very offended and if they think you're only interested in how much profit you can make, it will only make negotiations harder down the line. Less is more in this case.

If you think you might be interested, have a brief chat to the vendor to find out their situation – why they're moving and their ideal timescale – as that'll give you an idea of whether it'll fit with your plans and, more importantly, how far you might be able to negotiate on the price.

Second viewing

If a property stood up to your initial financial analysis, you liked the look of it on the first viewing and it compares favourably with the other contenders, book a second viewing. When you call to book, confirm with the agent that you've understood the vendor's situation correctly and tell them you'd like to take your time on this viewing. Call your builder and ask if he'll go along with you to highlight any potential issues he sees and also recommend and estimate the cost of any works. If your builder isn't able to go with you, try to take someone else who can be a second pair of eyes – you can research approximate costs later.

Go through each room carefully and make a list of all the refurbishment work you'll need to do. If the vendor's there, ask them when the plumbing and heating systems were installed and last serviced and how old the electrics are. Essentially, by the time you leave this second viewing, you should have a very good idea of how much you're going to have to do to get the property ready to rent.

Detailed financial analysis

This is the last step before you decide whether to make an offer and is really about confirming the price at which the deal stacks up for you.

Double-check you've factored in all the refurbishment items and got realistic estimates/costs for carrying out the work, then triple-check you've included all the other costs associated with the purchase and getting the property ready to rent. Check the ongoing monthly cost estimates, work the numbers on an average income situation (although you should be confident you can achieve well above average income!) and then also make sure you know what your 'break even' point would be as well as the maximum you can afford to pay.

You're almost ready to put together your offer...

Checklist

Researching and identifying properties

Have you done all these things?

Online research

- ☐ Established which local areas have the best demand v supply ratio for rooms
- ☐ Revisited local area research for future plans
- ☐ Confirmed specific tenant preferences for location and facilities
- ☐ Understand local market house price performance and established 'fair' purchase prices
- ☐ Have a good idea of current supply and demand for properties for sale
- ☐ Created a detailed spreadsheet to analyse costs, income and expenditure and KPIs
- ☐ Shortlisted at least 10 properties

Viewings

- ☐ Driven past before booking viewing
- ☐ Met with agent before viewing, to discuss requirements in detail
- ☐ Viewed once, checking for overall suitability and any major issues
- ☐ Established vendor's situation and timescale

- [ ] Discarded unsuitable properties and given agents feedback
- [ ] Viewed for a second time, preferably with a builder, and made detailed notes

Decision making

- [ ] 'Stress-tested' figures

Chapter 8

Making an offer

Before you make an offer, you need to make sure everything's in place, ready to proceed, and that you put together your offer in such a way that it has the best chance of being accepted.

Take the details of the property or properties you're satisfied will make good investments, along with your financial analysis figures, to your broker. They won't be able to make any promises, but should be confident you'll be able to secure financing for the purchase. People talk about 'agreements in principle', but the reality is that until you put in a formal application and the mortgage valuation has been carried out, there's no cast-iron guarantee that you'll get a mortgage. This is just one instance when you'll really see the benefit of having a specialist broker who has excellent relationships with lenders.

Instruct your solicitor (if you haven't already) and make sure you give them everything they need to be able to act for you – including documents that confirm your identity and any other instruction paperwork they require you to sign.

The other professional you'll need to source is a chartered surveyor who's accredited by the Royal Institution of Chartered Surveyors (RICS). Your mortgage lender will carry out a valuation, but you may need to instruct a Homebuyer's Report or Building Survey to get a more detailed report on the fabric of the property.

What should your offer be?

By now you'll have a very good idea of: a) what you think the property is really worth, b) the figure at which it works best for you without being a 'silly offer' and, c) how flexible the vendor is likely to be - and now it's a case of juggling those things and putting together a reasonable offer.

Yes, every property has a value, but there's also a value to time. You need to be able to judge your vendor, understand their position and then negotiate a price that means you feel you have a good deal, and so do they. If their time pressure is greater than their need to hold out for more money, and you can help them move on without ripping them off, that's a win/win situation. Similarly, if the vendors want to wait until they've found somewhere to move on to, and you decide you can work to a longer timescale, that also has a value.

When you put forward your offer, it's best to do it in person, either to the vendor or to the agent:

- Explain why you're making the offer that you are (local research on sold prices, level at which your business model works, etc.)

- Confirm your position: that your broker and legal representative are ready to act for you
- Suggest a timescale
- Confirm everything in writing

If the offer is significantly lower than the asking price, you don't want the vendors to be offended, so do make it clear to them that you're basing your offer on the price that works business-wise – you're not suggesting their home is vastly overpriced!

And one very important piece of advice: be sure you're prepared to proceed with this purchase, because once your offer has been accepted – regardless of the fact that you're not under any legal obligation – you've made a verbal agreement. In my opinion, that morally obliges you to see the deal through (unless, of course, you get an adverse survey that significantly affects the property's value). I said it earlier: your reputation is everything and you certainly don't want to become known as someone who makes casual offers or pulls out of deals, especially in the area where you live and socialise.

A good reputation can open doors;
a bad reputation will close many more.

If your offer's rejected...

...never go back to the agent immediately – take some time to reconsider the figures and your options. This is why it's a good idea to view ten properties initially: assuming you researched them properly before viewing, you should end up with two or three you'd be happy to proceed on. Always know your limit and be prepared to walk away from a deal if it gets too expensive or the vendors get too vague on the timescale. Your investment business plan will be based on a certain number of acquisitions a year and it's rare that you're able to be completely flexible on completion dates.

The first thing to consider is whether you're prepared to increase your offer. If so, you might choose to make it conditional, such as offering X amount more, provided completion takes place on or before X date.

If you're not prepared to pay any more, then explain why not and say you'll leave the offer on the table for a certain length of time (I usually give them a week), in case the vendor decides to reconsider.

If your offer's accepted…

Have a small celebration! Then you'll need to be like the conductor of an orchestra for the next few months, making sure your ducks stay in line.

Get things moving with your mortgage broker, who will make sure the lender instructs the valuation as soon as possible, and have your solicitor confirm to you that they've agreed the timescale with the vendor's solicitor. Most solicitors will be resistant to agreeing exchange and completion dates at such an early stage in the process, which is why you need to work with a buy to let specialist who understands the importance of keeping your plans on track. It's also worth checking out whether you can gain access to the property to start refurbishment work before completion. Most of the time this won't be possible, but there are exceptions and it's worth asking, as every day the property is untenanted, you're funding the mortgage repayment yourself.

You may think the property is completely sound, especially if you've had your builder give it the once-over, but for the sake of around £500, I'd rather instruct a Building Survey and find out about any hidden problems before my refurbishment team find them or – even worse – serious problems emerge once the property's tenanted.

You also need to meet with your project manager, go through the refurbishment plan (see the next chapter) and ask him to make sure his team will be available to start as soon as the purchase completes.

Speak to your local council planning department about your plans for refurbishing the property so you can make sure you're compliant with building regulations before work starts (your project manager may do this for you). Also, if you've been told you don't need either planning permission or a licence to let this property as an HMO, ask them to confirm it in writing. If you do need to apply for either one, then make sure you do that as soon as possible.

Complete, sign and return all paperwork you receive from your broker and legal representative right away and make sure deposit funds and fee and disbursement payments are all where they're supposed to be in good time. Although the estate agent (or their sales progression department) will be contacting your legal representative for updates on a regular basis, it's a good idea to speak to them yourself every now and then. Ideally, liaise with the vendor directly, so you can reassure them that everything's going smoothly and arrange any extra visits to the property you might need.

And, importantly, speak to a buy to let landlord insurance specialist – your mortgage broker will probably have a recommendation – to make sure you'll have the right insurance in place not only when you take ownership of the property, but when your tenants move in.

While every purchase is different, and the timescales can vary wildly, depending on the vendor's position and your own situation, you should expect the process, from offer to completion, to take around three months. Your conveyancer will be able to provide you with information about each step involved – familiarize yourself with it, so that you can not only make sure you're doing everything you need to, but also know where the other parties involved should be with their paperwork.

Checklist

Making an offer and buying a property

Have you done all these things?

Preparation

- ☐ Established vendor's position
- ☐ Met with broker and gained assurance you'll be able to finance the purchase
- ☐ Instructed solicitor to act for you
- ☐ Understood the steps involved in the conveyancing process
- ☐ Found a good local chartered surveyor

Making the offer

- ☐ Put it forward in person – to vendor or agent
- ☐ Confirmed in writing: offer amount, your position, suggested timescale

Offer accepted

- ☐ Make sure mortgage broker moves things along as quickly as possible
- ☐ Confirm timescales with solicitors
- ☐ Ask about gaining access before completion
- ☐ Instruct Building Survey
- ☐ Consult with project manager
- ☐ Speak with planning department of local council

☐ Sign all mortgage paperwork

☐ Sign purchase contract

☐ Get buildings insurance in place

☐ Transfer completion monies to solicitor

☐ Secure quotes for comprehensive landlord insurance

Chapter 9

Refurbishment

Assuming everything goes smoothly with the purchase, you should be able to collect the keys around lunchtime on day of completion. You now need to do everything you can to get paying tenants happily settled in their rooms as soon as possible, and that relies on meticulous planning. If you plan well and there are no unforeseen delays, I'd say you should be able to complete a fairly comprehensive refurbishment (gutting, updating plumbing and electrics, refitting bathrooms and kitchen, then decorating) in around four to six weeks.

Before you do anything else, go and introduce yourself to the neighbours and let them know that there will be work going on for roughly the next 4 weeks (or however long). Reassure them about what you're doing, and give them your contact details, so they can get in touch if they have any issues or concerns. Again, this business is all about relationships and taking the initiative in this way will be much appreciated.

Your refurbishment plan

Meet your project manager and his team on site to confirm exactly what needs to be done, map out floor plans and agree an achievable timescale. Ask them to supply written quotes and you might want to put together some kind of incentive scheme – perhaps that you withhold a percentage of the invoice until you're satisfied there aren't any 'snagging' issues after completion of the project, or a bonus for bringing it in on time and to standard.

All the contractors you engage MUST have the correct liability insurance and they should also be suitably accredited and/or members of relevant trade associations or bodies (see Chapter 6).

You then need to sit down and create a detailed written plan (I find a spreadsheet is best) that includes:

- every job required, broken down by room
- the contractor required for each job
- a schedule of works, showing the length of time each job will take
- all health and safety elements
- dates and times of deliveries of supplies/materials from external suppliers/contractors, e.g. carpet fitter
- Dates/stages when you'll need to adjust your insurance, depending on when the property's furnished and occupied

Go through it carefully with your project manager to make sure you haven't missed anything, and that he's also happy his team can work to the final schedule.

It takes a fair amount of work the first time you put one together, but if you take time to get it right, you'll have a great template for all future projects. I share mine on a cloud-based system so that everyone involved in the project can see exactly what stage we're at and I liaise regularly with my project manager in case any of the plans need revising as we go along. Also remember to update your financial analysis spreadsheet if any of the refurbishment costs change.

Health & Safety

Before you start any renovation or refurbishment, you must make sure your planned work is going to comply with Building Regulations. You should already have checked this out with the local council; if you haven't, then don't start any works until you have, or there may be penalties.

Then, even though you may be happy that you understand your health and safety responsibilities, it's a good idea to ask the local council Housing Standards Officer and Community Safety Adviser (or similar from the Fire Service) to come to the property while you're refurbishing it. You can explain to them exactly what you're doing, and make sure they're happy with your plans. You don't have to pay for this, and it avoids you having to possibly make changes at a later date.

Particular points to query with them are:

Housing Standards Officer

- Are the kitchen (particularly cooking) facilities suitable for the number of people?
- Are the room sizes acceptable (especially important if you're creating new rooms by putting up stud walls)?
- Are the proposed bathroom facilities sufficient?
- Are there any other facilities I should provide that I've missed?

Community Safety Adviser

- Is the fire alarm system (or smoke detectors) I'm intending to install acceptable?
- Do I need to put up fire exit signs?
- Are the fire escapes (which can simply be ground-floor windows that open wide enough and at the right height) acceptable?
- Where do I need fire doors?
- What fire safety equipment do I need in the kitchen? (usually extinguisher and blanket)
- Do I need any other fire extinguishers?
- What lock systems do I need on fire escape routes? (Your front and all other door/s must be able to be opened from the inside without a key.)

In terms of fire regulations, even if you're not licensable, it's sensible to ask a professional for their opinion on what's a reasonable level of safety.

Personally, I choose to err on the side of caution with health and safety. As I said earlier in the book, you have a duty of care to the people living in your HMO and need to take all reasonable steps to ensure they don't come to any harm.

Ask both the Housing Standards Officer and Community Safety Adviser if they'll come back once the refurbishment is complete and confirm their findings in writing. They may not – sometimes verbal advice is all they're prepared to give – but you should also ask one of them if they'd be happy to go through the fire risk assessment form for you. Again, they may not, but it's something that a suitably qualified professional should carry out, as they're better placed than you are to assess levels of risk. You may have to pay a Fire Risk Assessor to complete it for you, which can cost anywhere between £100 and £300 – not a great deal, in the grand scheme of things – and you can easily find a local assessor online.

Security options for room doors vary greatly, from Yale locks to code entry panels; you can also reduce the number of different keys you and/or your property manager have to hold. It's entirely up to you, but bear in mind that tenants will occasionally lose keys, lock themselves out and sometimes move out of the property without returning their keys, so you need to be able to gain entry and re-secure the property easily. Ask around at your local landlords association, and see what other people find works best, but if you do use keys, particularly for the main front door, I'd recommend you pick a system that gives you full control over who can duplicate them.

'Interior design'

This is where you need to strike the right balance between finish and budget. Your décor, fixtures, fittings and furnishings need to be hard wearing, modern and visually appealing, while staying within budget. An average of six people coming and going all the time means that, no matter how well you start out, your property is going to suffer quite a high level of wear and tear, so make sure carpets don't show dirt and stains easily, pick paint colours that will always be readily available, so that walls and paintwork will be easy to touch up, and make sure the kitchen and bathrooms are easy to keep clean. Most of this is common sense!

It's impossible to be prescriptive on cost, but I'd suggest you shouldn't spend more than £600 on furnishing each bedroom and make sure the furniture you buy for the communal areas is built to last…on the understanding that you'll probably have to replace most items every five years or so.

In terms of where you get the furniture from, it's a bit like finding good local contractors – there'll be somewhere in your area that deals in low-cost, sturdy furnishings, so ask around your team and other landlords. I have a great supplier, who now knows exactly what I need and can kit out whole houses for me, as well as replace individual pieces of furniture very quickly.

Minimum furnishing requirements:

Bedrooms: Bed with mattress, wardrobe, chest of drawers, curtain/blind

Living room: Sofa/s and/or chairs (seating for at least 4 people), table, television & DVD player

Kitchen/utility: Large fridge (6 shelves min), large freezer (6 drawers min), good-sized oven and hob, washing machine, adequate drying facilities (either a coin-operated tumble dryer or space for drying racks). Some landlords also install a dishwasher, but it's not essential.

You then need to stock the kitchen with everything you'd expect to find there - crockery, cutlery, glassware, cookware, utensils, kettle, toaster, microwave, etc. - and have an iron, ironing board and vacuum cleaner stored somewhere in the property. Essentially, all the tenants should need to provide for themselves is bedding and towels.

Finishing off and getting 'ready to rent'

Once the property is completely refurbished and furnished:

- Make sure your gas & electric checks have been carried out and display the certificates in the property – the kitchen is usually the best place
- Have the Fire Risk Assessment carried out by a suitably qualified professional, and take any recommended steps
- Install wireless broadband, making sure there's sufficient

bandwidth allowance to handle six people online at the same time

- Get the property thoroughly cleaned and arrange for an on-going cleaning service to take care of the communal areas – I'd suggest at least once a week
- Have a pinboard in the hallway or other communal area that clearly displays:
  ◦ fire escape information
  ◦ the property manager's information
  ◦ what to do / who to call in case of an emergency
  ◦ refuse & recycling calendar
  ◦ issue log, for your manager to see
- Make sure you have enough keys cut. As well as supplying the tenants with keys for the front door(s) and their rooms, if necessary, both you and your property manager should hold a full set and you're likely to need additional copies of at least the front door(s) for your cleaner and handyman, plus a set to give out to contractors.
- Ensure you've documented everything that's been done, and carefully filed all your receipts, as a lot of the work may be tax deductible
- Go back to the neighbours to let them know that work's finished, and thank them for their patience

Then stand back and see what finishing touches you need. Put up a few pictures in the communal areas, and also a couple of mirrors, which can really lighten up a dark hallway or landing.

Remember that the doors to the bedrooms will be shut all the time, and, particularly downstairs, where you've used what used to be reception rooms as bedrooms, that this can make the house quite gloomy. A mirror will reflect what light there is, and add a bit of depth to narrower areas.

And, lastly, while it's still looking brand new and perfect, try to choose a sunny day and take as many pictures as you can to use in your advertising – at least one of each room, including the bathrooms. More and more landlords are also making video 'tours' of their properties, so, if you can, do that as well. Take a few props to the house (bedding, lamps, plants, flowers, fruit bowls, etc.) to make it look homely, and make sure you get all the shots you need, because once tenants have moved in, it'll never look quite like that again!

Checklist

The refurbishment process

Have you done all these things?

Preparation

- ☐ Licensing secured (if required)
- ☐ Planning secured (if required)
- ☐ Compliance with Building Regulations established
- ☐ Informed neighbours about planned work / timescale
- ☐ Got written quotes from contractors
- ☐ Appointed a Project Manager
- ☐ Agreed an incentive / bonus scheme
- ☐ Created a detailed refurbishment plan

Health & Safety

- ☐ Met with Housing Standards Officer at the property
- ☐ Met with Community Safety Advisor from the fire service at the property
- ☐ Carried out Fire Risk Assessment
- ☐ Got all gas & electric checks and certification
- ☐ Chosen key system

Decorating & furnishing

- ☐ Planned a neutral décor
- ☐ Found hard wearing fixtures & fittings supplier/s

☐ Found a good local furniture supplier

Finishing off...
☐ Installed wireless broadband
☐ Found cost-effective energy supplier/s
☐ Had the property thoroughly cleaned
☐ Clearly displayed house, safety and local information for tenants
☐ Cut enough keys
☐ Put in 'finishing touches'
☐ Taken photos (and video)

Chapter 10

Getting tenants into your rooms

Part one: marketing your property

This is only a short section, because it's really not that complicated! There's the advertising and then the viewings and, provided your advert is good, and you 'vet' your enquiries properly, it shouldn't take very long to fill your rooms, particularly when the property is newly refurbished.

One bit of advice I'd particularly highlight is that there's no reason why you can't start marketing the property while the refurbishment is still going on. Obviously, wait until the walls have been plastered and there aren't wires dangling everywhere, so that it's completely safe, but taking enquiries a week or so before you're actually ready to rent can sometimes mean you already have tenants ready to move in on the day the work's finished. The downside is that you won't be able to post any internal photos on the advert, but don't underestimate the attraction of the prospect of fresh paint and a brand-new boiler!

Where to advertise

The vast majority of your target audience - young professionals - will certainly be searching online on SpareRoom, EasyRoommate and Gumtree. It's not cheap to keep adverts running and well-promoted, so while you're starting out, I'd suggest only advertising on one of those sites and doing it properly. Go back to your research, and see if one site shows a greater demand than the other, in terms of 'room wanted' adverts for your area, but SpareRoom is probably the best in your option currently. Put up as many pictures as you can, and, if you've been able to take video footage, put that up as well. The more of your property prospective tenants can see in the advertising, the more likely they are to feel positive about viewing.

You might decide to also try the local newspaper, but that can be quite expensive, so make sure you carefully track how many enquiries you get, and the quality of them, to see if it's really worthwhile continuing. I've certainly found that I get a high number of unsuitable tenants calling from newspaper adverts – unemployed, on benefits or with a child – and it wastes time having to deal with these enquiries.

If you have a hospital close by, see if the HR department will take your details and put an advert up on their intranet – sometimes larger businesses will also do this – but they may only work with you if you are a locally accredited landlord. If you haven't done so already, look into accreditation schemes, and see if you can enrol.

Handling enquiries

When you're first starting out, it's important to track where your enquiries are coming from, how many turn into viewings and how many of those turn into lets. You need to know which adverts are generating the right quality of responses so that you can focus on those in future.

Make sure you always take a full name and number, ask where they saw the advert, establish that they're in employment, and find out when they need a room, and for how long. You can then offer to show them the property.

'Selling' your rooms

You're not just marketing the property when you conduct a viewing as a landlord; you're marketing yourself. I've heard of people deciding not to take a room, not because there was anything wrong with the accommodation, but because they were put off by how the landlord behaved with them, so be aware of how you're coming across!

If they're keen to take one of the rooms and you're happy to accept them, you can then confirm the date they'd like it and the price, take a holding fee and make arrangements with them for moving in. Sometimes the first person to view a room will take it, but I'd say, on average, you need to conduct three viewings to secure a tenant.

What I would say is: trust your gut. If, while you're showing someone around, you feel unsure about them – for any reason, – then don't hesitate to put them off. The last thing you need is a troublesome tenant who either doesn't get on with the other house sharers or who stops paying rent, so don't feel bad about turning them down. Never accept a tenant you're not sure about, just because you want to fill the room – another tenant will come along soon enough.

Part two: checking your tenant out and checking them in

Referencing

The degree to which you reference your prospective tenant may be dictated by your mortgage lender, but may be entirely your decision.

If I was renting out a whole property on a single AST for at least six months, then I'd certainly carry out credit checks and take up references, but when someone's only renting a room in a house, it seems a bit of a waste of time. I take a month's deposit, ask them to complete a personal information form, and trust my instincts.

You can take a copy of their passport or driving license (but check how data protection regulations may affect you), and speak to their employer to confirm their status, but further referencing is simply not a good use of your time, and doesn't stop people disappearing without paying their rent. If you're in the HMO business, you have to accept that at some point you will be ripped off by a tenant, but it doesn't happen very often.

Before check in

Once you've received the holding fee from your prospective tenant, you can start preparing the AST. Calculate the deposit still owed and the remaining rent for the current month and make sure that the tenant is clear on the amount they have to either bring with them in cash on the day they move in, or transfer in advance.

The two other things it's important to make clear in advance are:

1. individuals' belongings are not covered by your insurance, so the tenant must make their own arrangements if they want cover
2. the TV licence only covers the communal area, so if the tenant wants to have a TV in their room, they're responsible for arranging their own licence.

Check in

If, for any reason, the tenant doesn't settle the full amount due, don't check them in, and tell them they'll have to rearrange for another day, once they do have all the money. As a general rule, when room renters fall behind with their payment, they rarely get back on track, so you absolutely don't want to start like that.

Assuming the money side is fine, go through the agreement, highlighting any particularly relevant conditions and restrictions, such as no smoking, notice periods and room access. Sign two copies of the agreement and have the tenant do the same. Confirm the monthly rent and give them a standing order form with your bank details on, for future payments. Always ask your tenants to pay by standing order – it's quick, easy, and it means there is a clear record on your bank statement. You can waste a lot of time trying to identify cash payments, sometimes not quite for the full amount, that appear in your bank without any reference.

Lastly, there's the inventory. Using an independent inventory clerk when it's only a room check in isn't really worth the cost, although you may want to use a clerk the first time so that you have a professional template. I now use an app on my tablet computer that allows me to take lots of photos and add written descriptions, then I email the whole document to the tenant.

Whatever you decide, you need to make sure you've detailed the condition of the ceiling, walls, floor/carpet, fixtures and fittings and all the contents. Any damage must be clearly specified, and I'd suggest you take a photograph of anything significant, so there's no argument at a later date. Also note on the inventory how many keys the tenant has been given and make sure you both sign the document. You must also give the tenant information on the scheme you're using to protect their deposit.

After you've checked them in and made sure they know where everything is and how white goods, etc. work, make sure you file all the paperwork, update your records and lodge their deposit funds with your chosen deposit protection scheme.

Checklist

Filling your rooms

Have you done all these things?

Marketing

- ☐ Started as early as possible
- ☐ Listed rooms on spareroom.co.uk (and possibly also uk.easyroommate.com and gumtree.com)
- ☐ Identified other advertising outlets that work well locally
- ☐ Set up a system for tracking enquiries

Checking in

- ☐ Taken holding fee
- ☐ Carried out referencing / identity checks
- ☐ Agreed move-in monies
- ☐ Gone through AST with tenant
- ☐ Taken an inventory
- ☐ Settled tenant in
- ☐ Filed paperwork

PART THREE:

MANAGING

YOUR INVESTMENT

Chapter 11

Managing your HMO

Once your property is tenanted, it needs managing – and HMOs more than any other kind of buy to let – so the key to doing it successfully is organisation. As your business grows, you'll be able to bring on staff to deal with the day-to-day management, but chances are you'll be doing it yourself in the beginning.

Your maintenance team

Having a good team of contractors is key to managing maintenance issues and making sure they don't escalate into major problems. When little things aren't fixed and tenants feel they're being ignored, it creates a lot of bad feeling, so you need to know your team will act quickly.

One of the most useful people to be able to call on is a really good handyman, who can take care of all sorts of jobs around the property, and also be the first port of call if there's a problem with the boiler or electrics, rather than you incurring a callout charge from your plumber or electrician. Tenants tend to be quick to complain without having a proper look at the problem, and it's often nowhere near as big an issue as they reported, or something they've inadvertently done, like turning off an electric oven at the mains socket.

Even if there is a serious problem and your plumber or electrician can't get to the property until the next day, sending your handyman round to give the tenants peace of mind that something's being done usually goes a long way towards keeping them happy.

And you can keep your team happy by paying them quickly. One of the biggest complaints you hear from self-employed contractors is about clients taking too long to settle invoices. If they know that you'll always pay when you say you will, and you don't mess them around, they'll be loyal to you. Thank them for jobs well done and make sure you remember them at Christmas time.

Regular checks

There are a number of checks that have to be carried out at regular intervals, so you need to set up some kind of diary alert to make sure you don't miss them:

- **Routine inspections.** You'll be seeing some of the property on a reasonably regular basis, as you check tenants in and out and deal with any other issues, but you should make formal inspections of the whole property at least twice a year. You'll need to give the tenants at least 24 hours' written notice that you're going to be entering their rooms, and try to do it at a time when they're not there, so you're not disturbing them. Note anything that needs updating, repairing, replacing or replenishing, so you can schedule the work, e.g. repainting a hallway or buying some more plates. Write to the tenants to let them know your findings, tell them about any work that's going to be taking place, and remind them of their obligations if any clauses in the agreement appear to have been violated, e.g. smoking in the property.

- **Fire alarm testing.** You need to test your fire alarm system regularly, note down the date and results of the test and keep the record separately from the property.
- **Gas safety check.** This must be carried out annually by a Gas Safe registered engineer, and the new certificate displayed in the property.
- **PA Test.** All electrical portable appliances (kettle, fridge, TV, etc.) must be tested annually by a qualified engineer.

Change-overs

You need to have a slick system in place for when one tenant moves out and another moves in, as it can sometimes happen on the same day. The outgoing tenant needs to be checked out against the move-in inventory, then the room needs to be cleaned and made ready for the incoming tenant, who must be checked in with a new AST and inventory. Again, it's down to systemisation, preparation and having a team you can rely on to get things done at the right time.

1. When notice is given, diarise move-out day

2. Confirm with tenant that viewings will be taking place and that they'll vacate the room by 12 noon on their last day

3. Check room to estimate any repairs/updating that will be needed

4. Confirm handyman (if necessary) for 12 noon on changeover day and cleaner for 2/3pm

5. Re-advertise the room

6. Confirm with new tenant that they can move in after 5pm

7. Prepare new AST and inventory

8. Take original inventory to morning checkout, go through it with tenant, agree any deductions from the deposit, take back keys and note a forwarding address

9. Handyman & cleaner prepare room

10. Check in new tenant with balance of move-in monies, AST, inventory and keys

11. Return deposit to former tenant and lodge deposit for new tenant

Obviously, if there are any serious repairs to be carried out, you might need to postpone the move in for a day, or agree with the new tenant what work will be carried out and when.

Even with the best preparation in the world, this won't always run like clockwork – some people are late, others are early – but I've never had any major issues. People are, for the most part, reasonable, and small delays can usually be smoothed over.

Refreshing and updating the property

It's generally the case that when you put someone in a nice environment, they'll treat it nicely. Conversely, if you put a tenant into a shabby property that looks as though you don't really care about it – maybe because you're not the one who has to live in it – they're not going to bother looking after it either.

You'll pick up things that need doing when you carry out your quarterly or six-monthly property inspections, but ask your property manager, cleaner and handyman to let you know if they think something could do with refreshing or replacing while they're going about their business in the meantime. Sometimes paintwork needs a touch up, the bathroom could do with a new shower curtain or a carpet would benefit from some professional cleaning. If you can make on-going improvements before the tenants even notice or think about mentioning them, they'll really appreciate it and, as well as treating the property well, they'll be less likely to complain about little things.

It's not just décor – refresh your appliances as well. If you buy the more budget-range kettles, toasters and microwaves, they may not be as hard-wearing as more expensive models, but you can afford to throw them out and buy new ones every couple of years. Regardless of how much you've spent on a kitchen appliance and how hard-wearing it is, when six people are regularly using it, it suffers wear and tear and starts to look shabby.

And it's the same with larger items of furniture. Budget on the basis that you'll probably replace sofas and armchairs every five or six years because, while they might still be usable, they'll be looking tired. If you want to keep charging top-level rents as more recently refurbished properties (including some of your own!) come on to the lettings market, you have to keep your HMO looking smart.

Handling tenant issues

Following on from what I said above, if you treat tenants with respect, they'll usually reciprocate. Of course, there will always be the occasional problem tenant, but there's a lot you can do to mitigate the chances of issues flaring up or non-payment of rent.

It really comes down to communication and ensuring the tenants feel they're being listened to – don't ever ignore a complaint. If it's a maintenance issue they're complaining about, then your contractors should be able to deal with that fairly quickly. If they can't, find out when they will be able to get to the property, and let the tenants know.

When a tenant is either consistently late paying their rent each month or has stopped paying altogether, it's important you don't let yourself get caught up in any sob-stories. This is business - you're not running a charity – and the tenant signed an agreement to the effect that they would pay their rent on time every month. Give them a few days to pay everything they owe, then issue them with a Section 8 Notice to Quit and start advertising their room.

Nine times out of ten, this results in the tenant leaving without any further discussion (and also without paying the rent they owe – but their deposit should go some way to reimbursing you for the lost rent), but very occasionally they'll dig their heels in, seek advice from an organisation such as Shelter, and refuse to leave. In that case, you can try to reason with them and assure them that if they leave you won't pursue them for what they owe; if that doesn't work, you'll have to begin eviction proceedings.

I'd strongly advise you consider using the services of an eviction specialist (or solicitor), rather than trying to handle it yourself. There is a particular order to the paperwork and a specific way things need to be done, and if you get one of the elements wrong, the tenant could claim illegal eviction, and you could be forced to begin the process all over again. For the amount they cost, eviction specialists are worth every penny. I should stress, though, it's extremely rare for a tenant in an HMO to see this all the way through to court – they're far more likely to back down and leave when they realise you're serious about the eviction proceedings.

What's sometimes more difficult to deal with is a serious problem between two or more of the house sharers. One of the most common complaints you'll get is about noise – one tenant being inconsiderate and repeatedly shouting, crashing about or playing loud music very late at night, disturbing other tenants. If it's several against one, then you can go ahead and give the culprit a warning about breaking the terms of their agreement, but if it's just one person's word against another, you can't be biased.

Issues like that can self-regulate – i.e. the tenant tones down their behaviour or chooses to leave as they're not getting on with the rest of the house – or the problem may need to be escalated. Don't hesitate to call the police if you're at all concerned about things getting out of control, and make sure your tenants know they can do the same. That might sound extreme, but you're a professional landlord, not there to arbitrate in personal disputes or take on someone who's causing a disturbance and possibly breaking the law. Having the police deal with these issues will ensure you and your other tenants aren't endangering your own safety, and make it clear to everyone that such behaviour won't be tolerated.

Checklist

Property Management

Have you done all these things?

- ☐ Have a good team of reliable contractors who'll act quickly
- ☐ Set up system for tracking regular checks
- ☐ Systemised the changeover process
- ☐ Recorded age and condition of all furnishings and white goods and prepared to update/replace them every 5 years or so
- ☐ Set up issue log for tenant complaints

Chapter 12

Managing your business

An HMO generates a lot of paperwork and relies on constant figure tracking and analysis, so it's imperative you have a good administration system and a good administrator to manage it. If that's not your forte, then employ someone who *can* keep on top of everything for you.

General administration

Filing paperwork correctly so it can be located when needed is something of a skill and if you don't do it every one or two days as your business grows, you can easily get in a mess (although some of this paperwork can be 'off-loaded' to a bookkeeper periodically). These are just some of the things you'll need to file:

- Purchase and mortgage documentation
- Refurbishment invoices and receipts
- Guarantees
- Utility bills
- Gas and electric certificates
- Tenant paperwork
- Rent receipts

- Bank statements
- Receipts for expenses
- On-going maintenance invoices

...and the list goes on.

Given that you're going to have an average of two tenants checking in and out of each room every year, you also need a good 'dead filing' system for archiving paperwork. As the number of properties you own grows, so does the paperwork, and you might quickly find that the area you originally designated as office space is a bit small! Landlords tend to start in a small box room, progress to converting the garage into an office, then realise they need other premises, particularly when they start taking on staff and needing more office equipment, such as better printers, a photocopier, shredder, etc.

KPIs

I said in Chapter 2 that I focus on three main things - profit, ROI and yield - all of which I'm constantly trying to maximize. Having systemised the business and taken on capable staff to essentially run the day-to-day operation, I'm free to do what I'm best at: ensure my investments give the best possible return.

Increasing profit

There are only two ways you can increase monthly profit: secure more rental income or/and reduce costs. Let's start with the slightly more straightforward one. You should have a complete breakdown of your costs on your main viability analysis spreadsheet, so it's simply a case of working through those and seeing if any reductions can be made, without asking anyone on your maintenance team to take a pay cut!

Your biggest monthly outgoing is always going to be your mortgage, but the costs of switching to a new product can be relatively large, so it's not something I do very often. I have a good relationship with my broker and am confident they're keeping an eye out for a deal worthwhile taking. What you need to focus on yourself are utility and telecom service providers and your insurance provider, and it really is worth getting new quotes every few months and regularly switching to get the best deals. A few pounds saved every month, across all the properties in your portfolio, can stack up to a significant amount every year.

Also keep an eye on your maintenance bills for repairing white goods, and make sure you don't end up spending more on fixing them than they're worth. Again, having a good supplier that you can trust to be honest with you about this is a big help. And don't be afraid to ask for discounts for buying multiple units. When suppliers know you're a landlord who's likely to be able to give them regular, on-going business, there are usually deals to be done with them.

When it comes to securing more rental income, there are three things I look at: increasing rents, increasing occupancy levels and renting things other than simply bedrooms:

1. **Increasing rents.** This isn't something you can – or should – do just because you think you can. While tenants will pay the best market rents for the best rooms, you need to make sure you don't price yourself out of the market. Keep an eye on what the competition is offering and charging because, while your refurbishment and furnishing might have made your property one of the best in the area when you started out, landlords are providing better and better quality accommodation as time goes on. At the same time, you must try to ensure you increase your rents at least in line with inflation, otherwise your profits are decreasing in real terms. It's a tricky line to walk, though, because you can only charge what people are willing to pay. My advice is to make sure you track the top, bottom and average rents in the area and be aware of inflation, so that you're always able to compare your returns accurately with both local averages and other investments.

2. **Increasing occupancy levels.** It's virtually impossible to consistently achieve 100% occupancy, but you should certainly be averaging at least 95%. As I've already said, voids will make a big impact on your profit, so you must do everything you can to avoid them. Retaining tenants is the cheapest and easiest solution, so make sure you fix problems quickly, take care of the property, and have a good relationship with your tenants, so they don't have any reason to leave your property for someone else's. People always move on at some point, but try to keep

each tenant for at least 6 months. When tenants do leave, try to have someone ready to move in right away, even if it means taking slightly less rent. That might be contradicting the last point (!), but you have to consider the implications of having an empty room for a week or two, 'losing' you rent, versus lowering the price by £5 or even £10 a week. It's almost always worth the slight reduction, not only in term of immediate rental income gained, but also because if you have rooms standing empty, existing tenants might start to feel there's something wrong with the property, and there's better to be had elsewhere.

3. **Renting out other things.** I know several landlords who make extra money from renting out garages and box rooms that are too small to use as bedrooms. That might be renting to current tenants or to other people - if something like a garage or storage unit is separate from the house. You can also generate additional income through having coin-operated washing machines and tumble dryers, although this has to be considered against the rent tenants are already paying for facilities. The point is, think laterally and make sure you're maximizing the potential of every square foot you've invested in.

Return On Investment

Increased income and reducing costs, as outlined above, will result in a better ROI, but you should also periodically look at the amount of capital tied up in each property and assess whether it might be worth releasing some of it. Back in the early 2000s, when the market was hurtling up, it was often possible to remortgage and release all the capital you'd originally put in – and then some. With the market the way it is at the moment, you're not going to be able to do that, but you could still get some money out after a few years.

In order to work out whether that's a viable and good investment move, your analysis spreadsheet needs to be up to date and set up with the correct formulae so you can immediately see:

1. With the increased mortgage cost, am I still achieving the monthly cash flow I need?
2. Will I be able to invest the money released in such a way that it gives a better return?
3. What is the cost (fees and other charges) of facilitating the equity release?

This is where, again, you'll realise the benefit of having a financial advisor who is also a property investor, because they'll be able to quickly work the figures, understand exactly what it is you need to consider and give you informed, relevant advice. Your knee-jerk reaction might be to say that you don't want to increase your mortgage costs because you need the monthly cash flow for income, but what if you could make as much or even more overall from reinvesting some of the capital in another property or even a different investment vehicle?

Ultimately, if you can get to the point where you have none of your own money invested in a property that's still giving you some monthly income, while also appreciating in value, you'll be getting an infinite return on investment.

Yield

Yield is the figure that allows you to see whether you're investing in the right kind of property – both in terms of type and location; gross yield is the rental income as a percentage of the property's value, and net yield is the profit as a percentage of value. I almost never look at other people's gross yield, because it doesn't take into account either how much money is invested or any costs, so is pretty meaningless when you're trying to compare two investments.

For example, because rental income is two to three times higher for HMOs than similar properties rented as single units, the gross yield is significantly higher. A detached house with four bedrooms and three reception rooms, worth £200,000 might rent to a family for £1,000 a month, giving a gross yield figure of 6%, while renting six individual bedrooms might achieve £2,400, giving a gross yield of 14.4%. But if the landlord of the single unit owns the property outright and therefore doesn't have monthly mortgage payments, while the landlord of the HMO is highly geared and has all the additional costs (utility bills, council tax, TV license, increased maintenance - handyman, cleaner, gardener - and more management costs), the net yields and monthly cash flow could be not that different. What will be very different is the ROI.

So I'd suggest you forget yield as a tool for comparing your properties' performances to other people's, unless you know that their investment model is the same as yours. What I use net yield for is comparing the properties in my portfolio with each other – that's where it becomes really useful, and it's something I'm constantly tracking. My costs don't tend to vary from one HMO of the same size to another, but the property values vary, as does the rental income. Looking at the net yield figures, I can see at a glance which properties in which areas were the better buys, from a cash flow perspective.

Of course, the caveat is that you have to take the yield figure in context with the capital growth figure. The yield figures might suggest you'd be better off selling a property and reinvesting the money into one that has a better income:value ratio, but if the reason for the lower yield figure is that the property has grown in value more than others in your portfolio, it's probably worth holding onto.

Capital Growth

Whether a property grows in value or not is pretty much out of your hands. Yes, you can make sure you maintain it well, and could extend, convert or renovate to add value, but once your HMO is up and running, it's in the hands of the market. Nevertheless, you must keep track of what's happening to property values, to make sure that you not only know how much your own portfolio is worth, but also can see which of your properties are growing more quickly in value.

As I said in the section above, you can greatly increase your ROI by refinancing and pulling out some of your invested capital, so keep track of exactly how much equity you have in each property, assuming you'll always need to keep 25% in. Set up your spreadsheet so that you can easily see:

- purchase price
- invested capital
- current value
- total equity
- amount you could pull out (total equity, less 25% of current value)

If certain property types in certain areas have grown more in value over the last few years, look at the economic drivers, and what's likely to happen in the future, and that will help you see whether it's worth making further investment there.

Most of the professional landlords I know keep a balanced portfolio, with some properties which generate a high level of monthly income and others which aren't so good on cash flow, but are much better in terms of capital growth. And I'd suggest that tracking your KPIs, so you can make sure you consistently maximize your returns in a variety of ways, and spread the investment risk, is a very sensible investment strategy.

One more little note…

Of these four key metrics, the one you'll hear investors most often mention is yield. What I'm saying is that yield needs to be taken as just one part of an overall picture which includes profit, ROI and capital growth, and it will be more or less relevant to you, depending on your investment objectives. So if someone says they're getting a better yield than you, understand that the conversation is only just beginning!

Checklist

Managing your business

Have you done all these things?

- ☐ Set up a good general administration system
- ☐ Made sure your property analysis spreadsheets are up to date & you have diarised:
  - ◦ cost reviews
  - ◦ current property valuations
  - ◦ rent reviews
- ☐ Understood your key KPIs:
  - ◦ profit
  - ◦ ROI
  - ◦ yield
  - ◦ capital growth
- ☐ Know what sources can quickly give you a snapshot of the current market
- ☐ Arranged with your financial advisers how often you will review your business

Chapter 13

In Summary

I hope this book has given you more than a flavour of what an HMO business is all about. What you should do next, if you haven't already, is go back to Chapter 1 and start putting some things down on paper. As you'll have gathered, the keys to successful HMO investing are research, planning and preparation, and all the professionals you'll be working with will need clear, detailed information about both your current situation and your future plans.

If you're not sure at the moment exactly what investment route to take, I guarantee you that getting the basics written down and asking yourself questions about what you want and need from the future – which you might not have done before – will help you achieve some clarity.

Go and talk to people who are already doing what you want to do, and achieving what you want to achieve. Good, successful businesspeople are usually generous with their time and knowledge, and will be happy to share their experiences. Network with these people and put yourself in situations where you'll learn more about investing, and HMOs in particular, and really think about whether it's the right business for you. There's a lot of hard work to be done, especially in the first couple of years, but as long as you have the right attitude, perspective and people around you, there's no reason why you shouldn't be successful.

"The only difference between successful people and unsuccessful people is extraordinary determination."
Mary Kay Ash, Entrepreneur

"Some people dream of success, while others wake up and work hard at it."
Sir Winston Churchill

"Your attitude, not your aptitude, will determine your altitude."
Zig Ziglar

While there's an awful lot to think about and do as an HMO investor, I want to leave you with the assurance that it's absolutely worthwhile – as long as you do it right (see Chapters 1-12!). Building an HMO portfolio has not only given me an excellent income stream and pension pot for the future, it's also introduced me to some incredible people and opportunities which I would never have encountered had I stayed in my previous software business.

And just to prove that, with the right team in place, your property business can run without you, I'm about to leave them to it for a whole month, while I take time out to holiday with my family! As I write, we're preparing to spend August in Ibiza, Majorca, Amsterdam and on a boat on The Broads. I'm just a phone call away, but I'm very much hoping it won't ring...

My life today is busier than ever, but 90% of the time I'm doing what I want, when I want, with the people I enjoy being around. My family is secure, I have great friends and a superb professional network and I'm able to give back time and money to help make a difference, in all sorts of ways.

"We make a living by what we get,
but we make a life by what we give."
Sir Winston Churchill

HMO PROPERTY RENOVATION & REFURBISHMENT SUCCESS

TAKING YOUR BRICKS AND MORTAR FROM PURCHASE TO READY TO RENT

About the co-author

 *Richard Leonard is a former technology project consultant with more than 20 years' experience in letting and managing property. Now a professional investor and project manager, he has a high income-generating personal portfolio worth over £3m and specialises in sourcing and refurbishing HMOs for clients in Hertfordshire.*

At the ripe old age of 12, Richard set up his first business venture, cleaning cars at the weekend for 50p each. He soon realised he was on to a winner when he had to recruit three of his friends to work with him to satisfy demand. "I can still remember how pleased and proud I was to have my old tobacco tin heaving with coins by the end of every Sunday afternoon. It was certainly a good business model: low overheads, great profits and loyal customers!"

After studying Electronics at Cambridge, Richard entered the corporate world and by the early 1990s was designing and managing infrastructure and I.T. projects for a number of global finance and technology companies. By the end of the '90s he had built a technology consultancy, which he continued to grow and manage through the '00s, delivering complex and demanding solutions to a number of large corporate clients, including Catlin, Eversheds, Barclays and Coca-Cola.

At the same time, he was investing in property. His great-grandfather used to work as a handyman for a local landlord and Richard remembered it striking him, even when he was a young lad, as rather romantic that this old man was keeping people's homes safe and sound. "I think it gave me a subconscious love of property and fascination for property management, and then when I read 'The Richest Man in Babylon' and 'Rich Dad, Poor Dad' in my early twenties, I realised investment was the way forward and that using property as a vehicle was the most naturally comfortable fit."

He teamed up with a business partner based in Luton and they began to buy property at auction, snapping up absolute wrecks for peanuts and doing them up. Buy to let mortgages hadn't yet been introduced, so they simply used Richard's capital and took out as many credit cards as they could, then let the properties out to recover their investment.

That was all at a time when the private rented sector barely existed. As there were hardly any letting agents in the market, Richard and his partner decided early on that they should establish their own agency, through which they could market and let their own properties and also satisfy a growing local demand for letting and management services.

Within two years, they had a portfolio of 300 properties and the business had got too big for Richard, who was still working his 'day job' as a technology consultant! In their third year, he asked his partner to buy him out.

A decade on, keen for another property business opportunity, Richard started up a letting and maintenance company, covering Luton and the Home Counties. This allowed him to once again indulge his passion for property on a part-time basis, as he continued his career with the blue-chips, but a few years later his world was turned on its head.

At the age of six, Richard's son, William, was diagnosed with a brain tumour. Treatment in London was unsuccessful, so the family was forced to temporarily relocate to Oklahoma, where specialised procedures would give William the very best chance of survival and Richard knew he could no longer commit to the corporate world. His accountant advised him that his portfolio was providing a good income and suggested he focused more on that. When William piped up from his hospital bed, "Dad, you should do the properties again", the future was sealed.

And so, in 2014, having already met Nick and several other professional investors, Richard founded Stevenage Lettings. The company lets and manages both Richard's personal portfolio and properties for other local landlords and clients. His HMOs give him a gross annual income in excess of £100k, with each property achieving a return on investment of between 12% and 16% - a return he consistently achieves for his clients.

"One of my main reasons for investing in property was so that I could establish a passive income stream that would pay for my day-to-day expenditure. I didn't expect to achieve that so quickly – HMOs have proved quite a revelation for me!"

With so many years of experience under his belt, Richard now has a specific template for sourcing, renovating and refurbishing properties, with a refined system and a trusted team in place to deliver it.

Richard lives in Walkern, Hertfordshire, with his family. He's passionate about his motorcycling and is an avid Chelsea supporter.

Preparation, Preparation, Preparation.
You can never do enough.

Introduction

People renovate and refurbish properties for two reasons: because it's necessary and/or because they want to 'force' an increase in the value of their investment. That may be their own home or a property they want to improve and sell on immediately afterwards, but in a large number of cases – and certainly if it's an investment – most people are making improvements because they want to let the property.

As you'll be all too well aware if you've read the other books in the 'Success' series, buy to let investing is a business and, needless to say, a property is only worth buying if it makes good financial sense. And the renovation and refurbishment is where too many people make mistakes, either because they haven't prepared well enough and budgeted correctly, which means their initial capital investment is far greater than they anticipated, or because they simply don't carry out the work properly. That leads to greater on-going maintenance bills and more complaints from tenants, which often results in a higher tenant turnover and not being able to achieve the expected level of rent.

Long story short, if you don't get this stage of your property project right, your whole investment plan can come unstuck.

How you renovate and refurbish will vary, depending on what you intend to do with the property. You need to be clear on your target tenant market and what they expect from their home, then make sure that's what you provide. And this isn't a process you can simply get right once and then endlessly repeat; demands and standards change as time goes on, so you must keep up to date with the market and constantly tweak, refine and update your methods.

For the purposes of this book, we'll primarily look at the process of completely renovating and refurbishing a property for letting as a House in Multiple Occupation (HMO). Needless to say, if you're preparing a property for letting as a single unit, not everything will apply to you - although most will, and it's worth getting an idea of what's involved in preparing a multi-let, in case you choose to go down that route at a later date.

PART ONE:

PLANNING, BUDGETING AND PREPARING

"Before anything else, preparation is the key to success."

Alexander Graham Bell

Chapter 1

Preparing yourself

Property is very different to most other kinds of investment because it demands a lot more from you, in terms of time, effort and knowledge. At one end of the property investing scale is the 'hands-off' investment, but even then you need to carefully research the investment provider, the investment itself and your finance options. At the other end of the scale is the entirely 'hands-on' investment – the buy to let property that needs a thorough overhaul - and that's what we're talking about here.

Each element of property investment is a small business in itself, so treat the renovation and refurbishment part as you would any other business. You need to think about what lies ahead and whether you're willing, able and prepared to take everything on. In most cases, when things go wrong, it's because people don't have the right mindset, so preparing yourself, mentally, for the project really is key. Here are the most important things to consider:

Do you know what you're letting yourself in for?!

The answer may be 'yes', but if you're reading this book, we're presuming it's at least a partial 'no'! As the saying goes, 'you don't know what you don't know', and the only way you'll find out what you don't know is by immersing yourself in the subject. So read some more books, search the web for information and, importantly, speak to other investors about how they tackled the process. Ask what things took them by surprise when they carried out their first renovation and/or refurbishment work and what they've learned to do better. Question them about the pitfalls and ask for advice on how you can do the best job possible. You can do all the 'paper' research you like, but there's no substitute for real-life experiences, many of which we'll be sharing throughout this book:

One husband and wife team we're working with at the moment are absolutely bowled over by how fast we're working and the level of communication we have with them and with our team. Renovating and refurbishing a rental property is a major commercial project, run in an almost military style, and when most first-time investors have only ever carried out works on their own home, it's quite a shift in mindset.

Do you know why you're doing this?

That might sound like an odd question, but we're always amazed at how many investors don't have a clear plan for their projects. What's your end-game, both in the short and long term? By that we mean:

a)   what do you intend to do with the property

once it's renovated and refurbished, and

b)   what's your exit strategy?

Property is just another money-making vehicle for us. What you ultimately want out of it (income or capital lump sum/s) and when (on completion of the project / on-going / in ten years / when you retire, etc.) will dictate what you buy and how you renovate and refurbish it, according to your target market, i.e. what kind of property, let in what kind of way will give you the return you're looking for?

So decide what your goals are and then spend some time carrying out specific local research. Use the internet to assess prices and demand (rightmove.co.uk and zoopla.co.uk have some great data you can access) and speak to local sales and letting agents to get their expert opinions on what people are looking for and how much they're willing to pay for it. Only then will you be able to decide what kind of end product you need to provide and what's going to stack up financially for you.

Are you prepared for the commitment you're taking on?

Anything that requires time, effort and money is a big commitment, personally, emotionally and financially. Investments always carry an element of risk and property is widely considered a 'medium' risk. If the amount of money you're putting in represents a large proportion of your overall capital savings, then the level of risk for you is probably higher than if you had a bigger 'cushion' behind you. And your attitude to this financial risk – potentially putting your own and your family's future security on the line - will affect you emotionally. We'll look at this in more detail in the next chapter.

If you're very hands-on with the project, it's going to take a lot of your time and you'll have to make sacrifices in your personal life. Hours that you might have spent watching your favourite shows, socialising and relaxing are highly likely to be given over to this project – are you prepared to knuckle down for as long as it takes? And, if there's a problem, are you in a position with what may be your other full-time job to be able to address urgent issues? If you have a salaried position with set working hours, you may find it hard to run a renovation and refurbishment project simultaneously, so think carefully about how much time you are, realistically, going to be able to dedicate to it.

Are you supported?

Following on from the previous point, make sure the people around you are also fully behind you. Your family and close friends are going to have to be supportive and understanding at various points and in equal measure, so talk to your nearest and dearest about what you're doing and be honest with them about how much time you're going to spending working and the extra pressure it might put on both you and them.

But it's not all misery! Share your enthusiasm, tell them when you've made good progress and then, when it's all over, you can celebrate with them properly and thank them for being there for you. Property investing can be a lonely and stressful business at times, so having the support of those closest to you will really make a difference.

Are you a decisive person?

Can you make a decision when you need to, or do you find yourself often thrown by having too many choices and tend to spend ages going back and forth? In this business there is a constant stream of options and decisions and you need to be able to, relatively quickly and painlessly, separate the wheat from the chaff, make a choice and move on. If you can't, you'll find your projects painful and stressful – and so will everyone around you!

We don't always make the very best decisions all of the time, but nobody's perfect. As long as you've carried out some good research and been diligent in checking out several available options, you can be pretty confident that it's at the very least a 'good' decision. Could you have made a better one? Perhaps – and you can improve on it when you carry out your next project.

How do you handle problems?

No matter how well you prepare and execute tasks and decisions, problems will arise. Property investment is a business littered with things beyond your control – tenant behaviour, forces of nature, market fluctuations – and the renovation and refurbishment process has its own share. Contractors will sometimes let you down; there may be an underlying problem within the structure of the property that didn't come up on your survey; supplies to the property may not be quite as sound as you thought; human error can occur; there may be an unavoidable delay with suppliers…and so it goes on. You need to accept that Sometimes Things Just Happen and, as with the previous point, you need to be able to assess what's happened, make a decision and move on.

So this is one of the key abilities you need to develop and a skill you need to hone if you're going to get involved in any project similar to this. It's the nature of the beast that hurdles will appear in your way and whether you succeed or not comes down to how you handle them. We've noticed that all successful investors have a common character trait where they almost relish issues and have creative responses ready to go. That's obviously something that comes with experience, but you need to try and fast-track yourself, mentally, and approach obstacles not just with a 'can-do' attitude, but also think ahead and anticipate those obstacles.

We were recently handling a project for a client where, once the sale had been agreed and we'd asked the council's HMO Officer to visit the property, she informed us that the kitchen was too small to comply with amenity standards. We knew immediately that we had two options: either take a wall down or to build on a conservatory. The wall would have cost £5k; the conservatory £3k, in addition to which, we knew that if we laid the appropriate foundations underneath the conservatory, that would be the groundwork done for a possible double-storey extension in the future. We were solving a problem in a value-oriented way.

What we're saying is, if you're the kind of person who gets flustered when things don't go to plan, you may find hands-on property investing tricky. But learning how to deal with problems more effectively is not hard if you put your mind to it, so it's worth having a look at some of the materials and courses that are out there. The one we'd recommend is a basic project management course called Prince2 (their website is prince2.com), which teaches you about the various aspects of managing a project, assessing and managing risk, and it's a really useful tool that you can use in many other aspects of your life.

Project management is about time, quality & cost and ensuring that triangle of elements is balanced, co-ordinated and managed effectively.

How are your admin and computer skills?

'Success' in the renovation and refurbishment business is defined as bringing in the project on time, on budget and up to standard and you can't judge any of that without a meticulously prepared initial financial plan and schedule of works. You need to be really organised and make sure quotes, invoices and receipts – of which there are a huge number! – are all correctly logged and filed, and you must be on top of the bank accounts and credit cards in and out of which all the money is flowing.

We try to keep it as simple as possible, so we and our team mainly use Excel spreadsheets to track all the money, time, activity and people. The only whizzy thing we use in addition is an 'illustrator' package (ours is compatible with Macs), into which we input all the information we gather, including photographs, and that helps us create the final 'landscape' for the project. You should be able to pick up a package like that for around £40, so it may be worth the investment if you're planning on carrying out multiple projects or, if like us, you end up carrying out projects for clients and want to be able to drag together information very quickly for progress reports.

However you record and store the information on your project, the most important thing is that your system makes sense to you. Don't be tempted to invest in a package that's counter-intuitive to the way you work – and we've tried a few like that! Many investors we speak to manage perfectly well with spreadsheets - you don't have to over-complicate things. You'll often need to access details and figures quickly, so it's important you're on top of everything all of the time and know exactly where to find the information you need.

If that doesn't sound like something you're good at or something you would enjoy, you might want to consider having someone else manage the project for you. You could have a personal assistant handle all the administration, but you need to understand the figures, the process and why the schedule is as it is and that's hard to do when you haven't prepared it yourself.

Again, there are courses and books that can help you become adept at all of this, but this business will be far easier for you to get stuck into if you're already organised, computer-literate and figure-savvy.

Do you have good people-management skills?

You're going to be dealing with a lot of different people throughout your project and it's important that you can not only communicate well and get on with them, but that you can keep everyone motivated and working to schedule. Property is a people business and by far the best way of getting things done is by making people want to work with and for you.

You need to be a good negotiator and reasonable; firm but approachable; clear and appreciative. You also have to be able to be the 'bad guy' when necessary and not hold back from getting rid of bad tradesmen or unreliable suppliers, and that requires self-assuredness and diplomacy. If you think any of that might be a struggle, again, it may be better for you to employ a project manager.

Are you ready for the buck to stop with you?

Most importantly - and you may think we're stating the obvious here - you need to understand that this property investment project is your business. You may employ other people to carry out various jobs but the buck stops with you. You need to be in control of the project all the way through and skill yourself up to handle it.

Ultimately, it's on your shoulders whether it's a roaring success or fails to perform as it should, so you must carry out due diligence every step of the way. We meet investors all the time who blame tradesmen, tenants, the market, bad luck….when the simple truth is that their property investment didn't succeed because of something/s they did or didn't do.

So that's the big question: are you ready to be entirely responsible for your own success?

You might think we're trying to put you off here, but that's not true. Renovating and refurbishing property is an exciting, rewarding and highly addictive process. When you stand back from the dust, bricks and mortar and compare the building you bought to the finished product, there's an immense feeling of pride and satisfaction. And, trust us, you'll want to do it all again.

DO

- **Ask lots of questions.** Talk to people who have achieved what you want to achieve and pick their brains.
- **Get yourself organised.** Brush up on your Excel skills, re-acquaint yourself with files and filing, get out your calculator and clear some office space!
- **Think about how comfortable you are with risk.** You're investing a lot of time, money and effort and there is a (very slim) chance it might not go quite to plan. Are you okay with that?
- **Research the market.** Know exactly what demand you're supplying.
- **Share your ideas and plans with those around you.** It makes the tricky days much easier and the good times a lot more fun!

DON'T

- **Overstretch yourself.** Are you absolutely sure you have the time and money to do this project yourself, properly?
- **Simply have faith that 'it'll be fine.'** You need to prepare thoroughly and then follow a process. You can't wing it.
- **Try to follow a system that doesn't make sense to you.** Ask people how they record and track figures, check out software that might help you, but it's not a 'one-size-fits-all' thing, so do what works for you.

Keep your first deal simple and take your time.

Chapter 2

Preparing your finances

Hopefully, you've already got your finances straight and this chapter should just be a little refresher. If, however, you haven't spent a huge amount of time thinking about exactly what you have at the moment and how you'd like your financial future to look, it's well worth reading one of the other books in our 'success' series, 'PROPERTY INVESTMENT SUCCESS', which looks at property compared to other investment vehicles and goes through the different ways you can invest in property to get different returns.

And if you haven't spoken to a financial advisor yet, make that your next move; even better, speak to a Wealth Manager, who can look at all your financial affairs and make sure that your investments complement each other and everything is working towards your financial goals, in the most profitable and tax-efficient way. That's likely to cost you more but, in our opinion, Wealth Managers are worth their weight in gold. Even if you already have a trusted accountant and are certain you know what you're doing, it's never a bad idea to get a second opinion.

The other person you absolutely must speak to – if your Wealth Manager isn't able to fulfil the role – is a property tax specialist. Tax efficiency in property investment comes down, in a large part, to how you split what's considered a 'revenue' cost item and what's considered 'capital' – essentially, is it something that's being carried out purely for the business of letting the property, or is it something that's an improvement, intended to increase the value? Some things are clearly one or the other, but there are quite a lot of instances where taking the right advice on what you purchase and how you allocate your expenditure can greatly reduce your tax liability, In short, don't scrimp on getting the right advice.

In this chapter, we're looking at the key financial elements you need to tackle – and this should all be done before you make an offer on a property. Far too many people find what they think is a bargain, or a 'great deal', believing that they can't lose, without having run any real figures. This is purely and simply a financial move you're making, so the decision as to whether a property is worth buying relies on a huge number of factors, including:

- The purchase price versus its real market value
- The amount of capital investment required
- Price growth projections for the area
- Current rental values
- Detailed income and expenditure projections for your particular type of rental
- The mortgage rate you can secure

Gathering this information requires a good knowledge of the property investment business, a detailed level of research and some careful budgeting, with best and worst-case scenarios. You need to be as sure as you can that even if things don't go according to 'plan A', you won't be left out of pocket, having to subsidise your mortgage repayments yourself, or, in the worst case, end up in negative equity, potentially having the property repossessed and losing all your investment. If you prepare your finances correctly, none of that should happen!

Researching property values and rents

There's a lot of detail about researching areas, property capital values and rent rates in two of Nick's other books, 'HMO PROPERTY SUCCESS' and 'THE SECRETS OF BUY TO LET SUCCESS', both available via nickfox.co.uk and Amazon.co.uk; suffice to say here, you need to do a thorough job. If your budget is going to be useful to you, the figures you're putting down for rental income and projected value, both before and after the project, must be realistic. For everything you do in your budget, you should know best and worst-case values and prices, and therefore what a reliable 'middle ground' is.

Look online, speak to agents and get out there and have a look at some properties, so you get a real understanding of what something at X price looks and feels like. As we said in Chapter 1, if this project is to be successful and financially beneficial to you, you have to immerse yourself in your local property market, so make sure you become an expert on prices and values.

Buy To Let mortgages

The two most important things to say about buy to let mortgages are:

1. Consult an independent mortgage broker. You need to know that the person you're talking to can access every product available to you in the market and that they're not restricted or biased in any way.
2. When you meet with your broker, go armed with a thorough personal financial statement and clear investment plan. Only by knowing exactly how much capital you have access to and what you want out of your investment, can a financial professional help you secure the right product for you.

It's a huge marketplace and there are thousands of mortgage products, but you may be restricted by how you intend to let the property (mortgages for HMOs in particular have very specific criteria), the condition of the property you want to buy and the type of work you're planning to carry out. And the type of mortgage that's best for you, in terms of deal/rate tie-ins and whether you go for interest only or repayment, will depend on your own reasons for investing and financial plans. A great mortgage deal for one investor may not suit another, which is why you need to take advice that's tailored specifically to you and your situation.

At the time of writing, the market for financing HMOs is a very small one and product rates currently range from 3.17% to 6%.

Although there aren't many lenders in this type of investment space, the ones that there are really understand what you're doing, so the actual application shouldn't be too painful for you!

We're often asked by clients whether there's any possibility of getting advance financing for building works, or whether they're likely to have retentions until any works are completed. The answer to both questions is 'no'. Most of the time when you're embarking on an HMO project, you're either buying an existing HMO to improve and upgrade, or you're converting a three-to-five bedroom family home. These tend to involve, at most, a few stud walls, perhaps the conversion of a garage or the addition of a conservatory or ground floor extension – things that aren't considered major building works by lenders.

We said it at the start of the chapter but, to reiterate: you must make sure you have funding in place before you start the project, so consult a broker at the earliest stage of your planning.

Investment Key Performance Indicators

Understanding the industry lingo and being able to analyse your figures accordingly will enable you to look at any potential investment and see not only whether it will give you the returns you want and need, but also to compare your proposed investment with others on a like-for-like basis. Once you know how to calculate Return on Investment (ROI), gross and net profit and gross and net yield, you'll be able to see whether you're keeping up with (and ideally exceeding) local market averages and how well your property/portfolio is performing against other types of investment. In short, you need to prove to yourself that a renovation and refurbishment project is the most appropriate place for you to put your capital. So here are those KPIs explained:

Return on Investment (ROI)

The ROI tells you what percentage of your invested capital is coming back to you each year in profit. The higher the ROI, the harder your money is working for you and the 'better' the investment. It's calculated by dividing your profit by your total capital investment (deposit, buying costs, refurbishment, furnishing, etc.). If you're intending to sell a property immediately after refurbishment, then it will be the profit you realise after selling and taking all the associated costs away. If you intend to keep the property and rent it out, you will calculate an annual ROI figure using the total annual rental profit. Clearly, in order to be able to do this, you need a clear and realistic projected income and expenditure budget.

For example:

Total capital investment	£75,000
Profit from sale (pre-tax)	£30,000 = 40% ROI
Annual rental profit from HMO	£12,000 = 16% ROI

And in case you're thinking that it looks far better to 'flip' the property in this situation, remember that you're getting this 16% every year from renting it out. In addition, because there has been capital growth, you may well be able to re-mortgage at some point and pull out some, if not all of your capital invested, which would increase the ROI accordingly.

This is the key figure that will allow you to compare your investment with others.

Gross and net profit

This is the annual rental profit figure mentioned above. Quite simply, your net profit is your rental income less your costs. You should also include an allowance for void periods (when the property/room is vacant) of around 5% and also for maintenance. We'll go into this in more detail in the next section, 'Putting together a budget'.

Your gross profit is simply your rental income, but this is not terribly useful, as costs are unavoidable but can vary significantly. This is one reason it's worth doing the best renovation and refurbishment job you can: so that you keep on-going maintenance costs as low as possible.

Gross and net yield

Yield is probably the figure you'll hear property investors talk about the most. It's also used by lots of companies selling investment deals, because they can make their headlines look good by mentioning fantastic yields, but keeping it very quiet that it's a gross figure, which is about as relevant as a gross profit figure. The only time gross yield is useful is in giving you a picture of which areas might have better returns, in terms of total annual rental income against the property value; otherwise it's fairly irrelevant, especially if you're trying to compare a property owned outright to one that is heavily mortgaged.

So, net yield is the annual net profit divided by the property's value, for example:

Property value	£200,000
Annual rental profit	£12,000
Net yield	6%
Annual rental income (before costs are deducted)	£26,000
Gross yield	13%

Once you've got all these KPI figures, you can then go out and make sure your investment in this project is a wise one, and you couldn't be making a better investment elsewhere. So, to make a start, you need a budget.

Putting together a budget, twice

This can't be stressed strongly enough: if you don't get this bit right, you could end up with, at best, a few unexpected costs and, at worst, a disaster of an investment. We're calling it a budget, but it's really more of an investment viability analysis, and we'd recommend doing it on an Excel spreadsheet.

It needs to show your income and expenditure, together with details of the property value, capital investment and mortgage repayment. You must also make sure you include allowances for voids and maintenance.

You're unlikely to find two investors who do their budgets and analysis in exactly the same way, but everyone will have more or less the same content. If you go to nickfox.co.uk and click on 'FREE STUFF', you can download a template; in the meantime, here are some of the key things you need to include:

Property details & initial capital input:
- The property's current value & a suggested purchase price
- Deposit required
- All buying costs
- Renovation & refurbishment costs (total from separate spreadsheet – see below)
- The cost of any mortgage repayments you'll need to make before the property can be tenanted

Projected monthly income:
- Your anticipated rental income
- Any other income (charges for washing machines or perhaps letting an outbuilding)

Projected monthly expenditure:
- Mortgage repayment amount

- Any utility or other property bills
- Maintenance costs
- Allowance for voids
- Management costs, if not doing it yourself

Renovation & refurbishment budget

This works here for your viability analysis and then together with your schedule of works (Chapter 5). On a separate spreadsheet, put together as detailed a list as you can of costs/expenditure required for the works and furnishing you'll be doing. The more detailed you make it, the more useful it will be to you, both on this project and in the future. Obviously, until you've actually secured a property, these figures will only be approximate, but research suppliers and talk to other local investors and get as accurate idea as you can of what are reasonable prices for labour and materials, etc. More detail about fixtures and fittings can be found in Chapter 8.

Very importantly, ALWAYS include a contingency. Things can change and problems can crop up and even the best-prepared budgets include a little wiggle room. We'd suggest allowing an additional 10% of the total cost you calculate for the renovation and refurbishment, so you don't hit a bump and find yourself short of funds. As standard, that's the amount we allow when we're putting together the first budget draft. Once the property has been properly inspected and the schedule of works drawn up, we pull the contingency down to 5% in the final budget. With every property, you tend to find issues that the survey didn't bring up - perhaps a flat roof is found to be leaking or there's some asbestos to dispose of – and it only takes a couple of things to eat into that contingency.

Only once you've been able to put all this information together in a budget will you be able to calculate your KPIs and see how well the investment project stacks up. Then you can start tinkering with the figures, seeing what changes or cutbacks you might need to make in order to get the returns you need and also how your proposed purchase would be performing compared to local averages. The more detailed your budget and analysis, the better you'll be able to see what you need to buy and how much it's worth spending on it in each case.

The first time you do the figures, you might feel like your head can't take it, but once you're clear on what you're doing and why, the next project will be far easier. As you go along, you'll tweak, refine and improve your analysis and, at the same time, you'll begin to recognise more quickly whether a property's worth taking on.

How we do it

We now have a pretty slick system for sourcing viable properties. Every week, two of us go out and view around ten properties that we've picked from an online assessment of 30-35 possibilities, where we've ruled out ones that don't meet basic criteria. For example, if any bedroom has a dimension of under seven feet it won't work; if any room doesn't have natural light, it's out. If we like one, we'll have a quick walk around to get a feel for the spec and an idea of how we could divide the space; things such as where we're going to put en-suites, where the soil stack is so that we don't have to use macerators and pumps, etc.

We then have a good chat with the vendor, go through our checklist and start to put together our statement of works: do we need a boiler and/or megaflow hot water cylinder, do we need stud walls, en-suites, and so on? Back at the office, we input everything into our software illustrator package, including all the photographs we've taken, to create a real landscape of the project scheme. It quickly generates the information we need to know about the extent and cost of works, the rents we'll be able to charge and gives us the bottom line figures: the monthly profit and the ROI. (See Chapter 5 for more information on compiling all your property information.)

And we're quite regimented in our decision on whether to make an offer. We look for at least £1,000 pre-tax profit per month and a minimum 12% ROI. If the schedule of works and income/expenditure projections stack up to satisfy those two bottom lines, our project is a go-er.

DO

- Have a clear financial statement, showing all your assets, liabilities, income and expenditure.
- Speak to an Independent Financial Advisor or Wealth Manager.
- Take specialist tax advice from someone who understands property investment and buy to let.
- Make sure you understand your KPIs and budget correctly. None of this is worthwhile doing if you can't assess how well your property project stacks up against other investment options.
- Include a 10% contingency in your initial budget.

DON'T

- Forget to make sure your capital is accessible. A project can be lost through capital not being available in time.

And, very importantly…

DON'T forget to put a value on your own time. We say it over and over: there are too many investors who think they're saving money by doing things themselves that actually turn out to be false economy. Every hour that you're working on this project is an hour you could be doing something else and you need to look at the cost of getting someone else to carry out the work versus the value to you of having that time to yourself – whether you used to earn more in your 'day job' or simply think it's more valuable to you to be able to spend more time with your partner. Keep track of how long you spend on the project so that when it's over, you can look at your returns and profit and decide how worthwhile all the investment of your time has been. Your time is a KPI too.

If you have any queries about how to find good advisors for your property investment business, just email hello@nickfox.co.uk and we'll be happy to point you in the right direction.

Chapter 3

Preparing for the legal bits

Buy to let is full of legal requirements and regulations, some of which can feel as though they're getting in the way of your project, but it really is important you adhere to all of them. And you can't adhere to something you don't know about, so this is where you really need to make sure you dot the 'i's and cross the 't's, as the legal pitfalls of renovation and refurbishment can be deep - expensive and with serious repercussions. Most relate to planning, building standards and health and safety and, while some are national regulations, many can vary from area to area, so the first place you need to acquaint yourself with is your local council office.

And that's a little more time-consuming than you might have hoped, because departments rarely share information, meaning you have to liaise and build separate relationships with each one. There's really no way around this, but if you make a good job of it with your first project, your second should be a whole lot more straightforward.

If you're not used to dealing with these kinds of legalities and processes – and particularly if you've never had to work with your local council - many of the conversations you have with council representatives and planning professionals will feel frustrating, because it's very tricky to get anything in writing. Of course, all your formal applications will be acknowledged in black and white, but final decisions will take time to come through and, nine times out of ten, what you're looking for is an immediate yes or no! So, successfully navigating your way through the early stages, where nothing can actually be put in writing because you may not have a property yet, becomes heavily reliant on you laying the groundwork and building good relationships with the people who have the answers – or at the very least an informed, 'inside' opinion. You need to get yourself to the point where they understand what you want to do, you understand what you need to do for them and you know that they'll give you as reliable an indication as possible as to whether you're likely to get a yes or a no in a particular situation.

If we're making it all sound a bit 'grey', that's because it is. Of course, there are certain things you have to do and certain things you can't do, but much depends on how well you explain and provide supporting materials for your plans; much is dependent on the market conditions at the time you submit your paperwork and much is dependent on how the person making the decision feels on the day. It's a bit like taking an exam: if you've done your homework properly, there shouldn't be any surprises, but nothing is guaranteed.

The good news is that you're one step ahead of the game reading this! Here are the key legal pools you're going to be wading through during the successful execution of your project, together with the main points you need to consider and how best to address them.

Planning permission

Planning doesn't only relate to new buildings, conversions and extensions; it also covers change of use. This is of particular relevance if your project is the conversion of a single-household home or block of units into an HMO, as the rules governing change of use from one 'class' of housing to another (primarily C3 to C4) changed in 2010.

The national law states that a property will simply automatically change class as it changes use but, in practice, that's rarely the case. And that's because each local Planning Authority has the right to make an Article 4 Direction, which requires anyone wishing to let a property as an HMO to apply for planning permission. Many council areas have chosen to go down this route, as it enables them to ensure no one area becomes saturated with this particular type of accommodation. While that broadly makes sense, it does make things more difficult than they used to be for you, as an investor:

a) Before you commit to investing in an area, you need to check whether the local planning authority has an Article 4 Direction in place and find out, by speaking to them directly and talking to other local landlords, how they tend to rule.

b) If there is an Article 4 Direction in place, you could find yourself having to complete on a property before you've had planning approval for its use as an HMO signed off!

c) Because regulations are constantly shifting within the sector, you need to make sure you have the right contacts to keep up to date with any changes that might affect you.

So, if you're looking to let property as an HMO, make an appointment to see your local HMO Officer / Amenity Standards Officer (the title may differ between local authorities) to find out exactly what their HMO policy is and which areas it could prove tricky for you to invest into. These people are there to help you, so use them! Be up front about your intentions and ask for their advice, making it very clear that you're a professional investor, looking to provide high-quality accommodation that helps fulfil the local housing needs in the best way.

If, in doing that, you're going to be extending or converting part of a property – which is highly likely – you also need to speak to the local Planning Officer to find out what kind of projects tend to be approved and which are usually turned down. The more specific you can be, the more seriously they'll take you, so make sure you've carried out proper research into the rental demands of the area and can demonstrate that your plans are intended to satisfy those demands.

Most of the work we do in our renovation projects falls under 'permitted development', which mean you don't need to make a planning application. Loft conversions or changing a garage into a room, for example, are usually permitted development but, as with so much of the legislation around property, it does vary between councils.

We always get in touch with the local council planning office prior to purchase, to discuss our plans and check what's within permitted development. For any proposed works that fall outside that, we find out about the likelihood of planning being granted, so we know at the earliest stage what changes we may need to make to our schedule of works.

For example, last year, we had agreed the purchase of a fairly modern property that we wanted to convert into an HMO, but the local planner wouldn't allow a carport to be built up and converted into a room. The reasoning was that it would remove a parking space for the property, something that's often an issue with newer properties, particularly if they're within an estate. Not being able to convert the carport took our plan down from a six to a five-bedroom HMO. Fortunately, we were able to add a single-storey extension to the rear so that the figures still stacked up, however, that could easily not have been the case.

In addition to the council planners, you should also be able to find freelance planners to advise and act for you. They tend to be people who used to work for the local council and who therefore know how the system works and who to go to within the council to get the answers you need. You will need to pay for their services, but it may be worth the investment for peace of mind and to have someone who can expedite any planning applications for you.

Building Regulations

Hand in hand with Planning Permission comes Building Regulations. Most aspects of your refurbishment project will require the approval of a Building Control Officer / Building Inspector, who will work with you and your contractors to make sure all the work is up to standard. As with HMO Officers, these people have an advisory role and are there to help you, although you will have to pay for their services – usually somewhere between £400 and £800, depending on the extent of the works and number of inspections required.

We sit down with the Building Control Officer as soon as we start the project and show them what we're planning to do. We agree a fee for a series of inspections that will take place at various stages of the project, creating a Building Notice, which includes a final inspection for sign-off. At the end of the project, you'll be given a certificate to say everything's been done correctly, giving you peace of mind that there won't be any come-back at a later date.

Soundproofing within HMOs is not something that's required as standard, but it has come up a few times as an issue for Building Control in certain local council areas. This is something that can cost tens of thousands to rectify if you have to install it retrospectively, so make it very clear how you intend to let the property and ask the officer the question about soundproofing, even if they don't bring it up.

Health & Safety

Much of this concerns fire safety, so, if your HMO / Amenity Standards Officer can't advise you, have a conversation with your local Fire Safety Officer. Every fire department should have someone who will happily advise you, completely free of charge, as to what you need to do to be compliant. Explain to them how you intend to let the property out and they'll be able to give you guidance about what you should install in the way of:

- Fire alarms
- Smoke detectors & heat sensors
- Fire doors
- Fire extinguishers & blankets
- Exit signs and other signage
- Windows at the correct level to provide escape routes
- Emergency lighting.

How much of the above you're legally required to do will depend on whether your property falls under HMO licensing legislation. But, regardless of what the law dictates, it's always best to err on the side of caution. Lettings legislation is constantly being amended and updated, so try to stay one step ahead by going the extra mile right from the start. Installing these safety measures is much easier to do at the renovation and refurbishment stage than at a later date.

You will also need to carry out a fire safety risk assessment, analysing the potential hazards in the property and declaring that every reasonable step has been taken to avoid them. There's nothing to say you couldn't do this yourself, but we wouldn't advise it, unless you can prove you've been properly trained in fire safety. This is a document that you might need to rely on, should anything happen to one of your tenants in the future and they accuse you of negligence. Paying a couple of hundred pounds to have a professional complete the assessment for you is money well spent, in our opinion.

The other thing you need to look into, particularly if you're going to be splitting rooms and putting up stud walls or converting spaces into bedrooms, is the minimum room size requirement. Your HMO Officer or someone from the Housing Standards department will be able to advise you on how many square meters you need to provide as a minimum in order for a room to qualify as single or double, and they'll also give you guidance on the amount of cooking, refrigeration and washing facilities you should be providing, according to the number of tenants you intend to house.

Again – and we're going to keep saying this! – standards will vary between councils. The information will be available on their website, so start off by looking there, so that when you do speak to someone in the department, you're already armed with some knowledge and can demonstrate that you're keen to make sure you're compliant.

We've heard lot of horror stories about people who'd mistakenly thought they could save themselves a lot of aggravation by 'flying under the radar' with the local council but, in almost every case, they ended up losing time and money through having to retrospectively comply with planning, building or health and safety regulations. It's really not worth the risk and, with the private rental sector continuing to grow, you really need to make sure you're above board with everything you do, so that you can confidently charge a good level of rent.

Landlord accreditation

Currently, there is no legal requirement for landlords in England to be either registered or accredited/qualified in any way. However, given that landlords in Scotland and Wales do now need to register themselves and/or their properties in order to let legally, we're of the opinion that similar legislation is likely to hit England in some form in the next few years. So we'd recommend you check with your local landlord's association whether they offer any kind of accreditation. Sometimes the checks made on you for accreditation are not particularly thorough, but we'd always suggest you show willing.

Also, check with your HMO Officer or Amenity Standards that you're on any register they might have for HMOs. This is something quite separate from licensing and most councils will make a note to carry out inspections every few years, just to check that your fire safety standards and amenities continue to meet the minimum requirements.

Insurance

At the point at which you exchange contracts, you will need to have buildings insurance in place, and that's the case regardless of whether it's residential or buy to let. However, as a landlord you will need specialist landlord insurance and, if you're letting an HMO, you're likely to be very limited in your choice of providers. We use 'block insurance', where we have one policy that covers our entire portfolio of properties and every time we buy a new one, we just add it in. It's cost-effective and cuts down on the admin, which, in itself, saves money.

The important thing with insurance is to communicate exactly how you'll be renting the property out and make sure that you're covered for absolutely everything you might need. As a landlord, in addition to standard property concerns such as fire, flooding, theft and accidental damage, you should certainly be asking about cover for:

- Professional indemnity (protecting you against any claims that might be made by tenants, visitors or contractors for personal injuries sustained in the property)
- Malicious damage by tenants
- Re-housing costs (giving tenants somewhere else to live while any repairs are taking place)
- Rent guarantee insurance.

And speak to your insurer about the planned works and how long they'll take to complete, because they will want to note when various stages are taking place, when the property is occupied, how it's secured during works, etc., and they might want to come out and inspect the property. They may even ask to see your schedule of works. In short, be very open about what you're doing and volunteer as much information as you can, because the last thing you want is for something to go wrong during your project and to find out you're not covered because of something you failed to declare to your insurer.

In addition, you MUST make sure that your contractors have their own appropriate public liability insurance. Some will also hold professional indemnity insurance that covers their work, and you need to check their health & safety process – how do they ensure the site is safe and can they demonstrate that they're working in a safe way? We'll come on to checking credentials and go into more detail in the next chapter…

DO

- Present yourself as a professional 'career' investor. Show you understand the local market and intend to provide high-quality accommodation that complies absolutely with letting regulations and exceeds expectations.
- Make sure you can demonstrate that your project will satisfy local demand. When speaking to the local council, show that your project has a clear purpose and will be beneficial to the area.
- Speak to local Amenity Standards / HMO, Planning and Building Control Officers at the earliest opportunity.
- Be very clear with your insurer about what you're doing and when.

DON'T

- Put any offers in until you've spoken to the council to find out what you can and can't do. The last thing you want to do is end up with a property you can't transform into the money-making vehicle you'd planned on having.
- Scrimp on paying for planning and building control advice. Doing a good job of building relationships with these professionals from day one will pay dividends in the future.

Tip...

You will be able to view and/or download both the minimum amenity standards and fire safety standards from your local council website, under the section on Private Sector Housing / HMOs.

Chapter 4

Preparing your team

Having a good, reliable team to carry out the work for you is probably the most important factor in the success of the project, after your financial budgeting. Remember the 'triangle' of time, quality and cost that we mentioned in Chapter 1? If any of your team of contractors, suppliers and professional advisors doesn't do their job properly, all three of those things are affected. In this business, you're relying a great deal on other people doing what they say they can do, when they've said they'll do it, to the standard you require and at the price they've quoted. When you take those four requirements and multiply them by the number of people on your team, that's a lot of risk.

So preparing your team is about two key things: finding the right people to work with and establishing a great line of communication with those people. It's about researching their credentials, making it very clear what you expect from them, right from the start, and then managing them in such a way that you get the best out of them. You might not get it right the first time and you will almost certainly have to let people go and find better replacements every now and then, but that's just another one of the hurdles this business throws at you. The key is being able to deal with it and move on.

Good property tax advisor

Everyone on your team is important, but a good property tax advisor is the person who can ultimately make a very big difference to the profitability of your investment, year after year. The renovation and refurbishment stage, which involves probably the greatest capital outlay you'll make on the property, is where your expenditure really needs to be allocated in the right way. We'd suggest that only someone who is both highly qualified AND has years of experience of handling the tax affairs of buy to let investors can advise you properly.

And this is someone you ideally want to engage before you buy any properties, because they'll also be able to advise you on the best way to own your investment/s, depending on what returns you want from them and when, to suit your income, capital, inheritance and retirement planning.

Where do I find this person?

Take recommendations from other investors, ask around at your local landlords association....your independent financial advisor should also be able to give you some recommendations. Ideally, choose someone who's an investor themselves – preferably with HMOs or, at the very least, with clients who have HMOs. You want to engage someone who knows exactly what they're doing and if it costs you a little more than you'd hoped, we'd suggest that paying extra for the additional expertise is probably worth it.

Pro-active mortgage broker

This may be a mortgage broker, it may be an independent financial advisor, but whoever is arranging your mortgage for you, make sure that they're completely independent and can access every product available. It's also hugely important that they're pro-active and will keep you informed about any upcoming changes to your product, anticipate when fixed rate or discounted periods are coming to an end, and always be on the lookout for a better product. You should be speaking to your broker around once every six months, just to make sure everything's in order and to get their thoughts on how the market might shift in the next 6-12 months. Your mortgage repayment is your biggest monthly cost, so making sure you're always on the best available rate can really make a difference to your on-going profits.

Local authority officers

As we said in the previous chapter, you should build good relationships within the relevant departments at your local council and consider them part of your wider team. The three key people you need to have on your side are:

- Planning Officer
- HMO / Amenity Standards Officer
- Building Control Officer / Building Inspector

With each of them, it's important that you present yourself as professional and informed – the easier you can make it for them to deal with you, the more willing they'll be to help you out when you need it. So have to hand simple copies of your schedule of works, together with sketches and any other pertinent details of the property. Make sure you've looked at the local council website and spoken to other local landlords before you meet with these council officers, so that you have a fairly good idea of what they're going to say and can prepare specific questions.

These people are there to help you achieve a good standard of work and provide high-quality rental accommodation. They're not trying to be deliberately awkward – remember, there is still a huge undersupply of private rental sector properties, so they want you to invest in the area – so if they're asking for certain things to be done a certain way, it's because they're looking to maintain standards. And be pro-active when you speak to them. Don't just find out what you're obliged to do and what the minimum standards are, ask them their opinion on what they think would be ideal. Show them you're keen to exceed expectations for quality and safety and they'll be keen to encourage you in return.

The caveat to the above is that sometimes you need to stand your ground. For example, you might be told that you need to put a washbasin in each room, or that a second cooker is required when, really, common sense tells you that it's just not necessary. As much of the amenities advice is guidelines, rather than law, you can often argue your case successfully – provided that you have a good relationship with the officer and can show that you've taken every step to comply with all the legal requirements, going over and above in some cases.

Essentially, you need to demonstrate that you understand the local authority regulations and guidelines and make them see that you want to work with the various council departments to help raise the standard of accommodation in the private rented sector. Some of that is down to research and preparation; some is down to your interpersonal skills, so make sure you've done all you can to hone both.

Contractors

It's really important you get your team of contractors right, because they have to work together. Over the course of the renovation and refurbishment project, things have to be done in a certain order and if one of the tradespeople is running behind, it can throw out your schedule of works (see the next chapter), plus, if the team don't get on with each other, it makes for a bad atmosphere and negative behaviours. We'll come on to talking about managing the team shortly, but, when you're selecting your contractors, bear in mind that it's not just the quality of their work and price you're looking at, but their overall reputation for having a good attitude on site.

These are the key players you'll need on the team, together with the associations and/or trade bodies they should belong to:

- Builder / Lead contractor (ideally, someone who can also project manage), preferably a member of the Federation of Master Builders (FMB)
- Plumber, Gas Safe registered
- Electrician, 'Part P' registered
- Plasterer, preferably a member of the Federation of Plastering and Drywall Contractors (FPDC)
- Painter/decorator, preferably a member of the Painting and Decorating Association (PDA)
- Glazer, FENSA member
- Locksmith, ideally from the Master Locksmiths Association
- Carpet fitter
- Cleaner.

Where do I find these people?

Checkatrade.com is a great source and take recommendations from other local property professionals. Your suppliers will also be able to give you leads, so keep asking around and you'll find the same names will come up. Then it's a case of meeting face to face to talk through what you'll need and ask to see examples of their work. And if someone's busy, that's good – always be wary of a contractor who doesn't yet know you but seems to be able to do anything you want as soon as you want it!

Although we've already mentioned it above, we just want to stress how important it is that before you engage any contractor, you check their registration with a relevant organisation / trade body and that they have the appropriate insurance. You must be sure that if anything goes wrong or you're not happy with their work, you have some kind of recourse. If you've taken recommendations and testimonials, you shouldn't find yourself with any cowboys, but do double-check online that they really are paid-up members of the bodies they say they are.

Managing the team

You may be tempted to project manage the refurbishment yourself, but I'd highly recommend you employ someone else to do it. The refurb contractors need to be able to work together – if they all have their own agendas, you can find projects stall or take longer than necessary because they're all blaming each other for not being able to get on to the next stage. A project manager (often a general builder) will usually have a regular team that he knows will work efficiently together and you pay him extra to make sure everything stays on track. It also means you only have one person to liaise with.

Right at the start of the project, we get all the trades together for a meeting on site and go through everything on the schedule of works to make sure the whole team's clear on what they're doing and the fact that the lead builder is responsible for the day-to-day management of the process. You'll still need to be on site regularly yourself to check everything's going as it should; this is your project and it's ultimately your responsibility to make sure the team is happy, working to standard and there aren't any problems, so don't think you can put your feet up until the project manager says it's all done!

In terms of getting the team to work well for you, it's quite simple: pay them on time and be considerate, be human. Our team get regular work, we give them 40% up front and pay stage payments when they're due. We don't mess them around and usually arrive on site with sandwiches, biscuits and a good sense of humour. Yes, you need to keep things moving along and address problems, but remember these are just people earning a living, like you, so treat them well.

Suppliers

In the main, your contractors will provide their own materials and will certainly be able to recommend suppliers that they're familiar with for the fixtures and fittings you'll need to choose. However, it's always worth getting further quotes and looking at other suppliers. As with much of this business, there will be certain places that are used to supplying buy to let properties, so you'll probably get the most appropriate recommendations from other local landlords and the contractors who are used to working with them.

We let all our tradesmen get their own materials – it's much easier that way. However, you do need to make sure that they know to break down all the materials and labour and list them separately on their invoices. Your tax advisor can't do their job properly if the figures aren't where they should be.

Remember also that if you're going to be furnishing a property, some items may need to be ordered and could have a long lead time, so make sure you find out how long things like bathroom suites, beds and sofas might take to arrive. The last thing you want is to have the fabric of your property all ready to go and beautifully decorated, then end up paying the mortgage for another month because you can't tenant your HMO unfurnished!

Utility providers

They're not, strictly speaking, part of your team, but they are important suppliers and choosing the right provider/s can really make your life – and your tenants' lives – a lot easier. We use a company that specialises in shared housing and supplies all our utilities (energy, water, phone/broadband & TV licence) under one umbrella. The huge benefit is that there's a single bill per month, per property, which cuts down massively on admin, leaving only the council tax on top to worry about. You don't want multiple bills on same property - that's just an unnecessary time and money overhead - so we'd strongly recommend going with a specialist provider like this.

Letting agent

If you're intending to use a letting agent, you must include them in your project and ask for their advice. In carrying out your initial research into local demand, you'll probably find you click with one agent more than others; not every agent really understands buy to let and property as an investment, so you might need to speak to more than one person in a branch to get the information you need about yields and returns. Even if you're not planning to use a high street agent to let the property, or engaging a freelance property manager, it's still an idea to build a good relationship with someone local, who can help you stay on top of tenant demand, wants and needs.

When you do find someone who 'gets' what you're doing, be proactive in your communications with them. Letting agents often get a heads-up when landlords are selling, before properties go on the market, so let them know you'll view on a phone call, without necessarily having seen details, always turn up and always call them soon afterwards to give them your feedback.

Most good agents will be happy to help out local landlords, so tell them you'd really appreciate their advice. Show them the property at an early stage, check that your original research is still correct and find out exactly what tenants are currently looking for, in terms of décor, furnishings, etc. This doesn't change very much over time, but there may be something that the agent finds tenants are suddenly asking for, such as satellite television or more washing machines, and they'll be able to advise you as to what extra things you might be able to include that will make the rooms let more quickly and/or enable you to charge more rent. You can then go back to your budget and financial viability spreadsheet and see if it's worth doing.

In short…

…preparing your team is about research and communication. Be very clear on your goals and plans, take the time to find the right people for you and then communicate with them exactly what you need and expect. If you've prepared yourself properly, you shouldn't find this too difficult.

DO

- Check the credentials of your team. Sometimes people have let their certification or trade body membership lapse; sometimes they lie – you should be able to check them all out online.
- Be clear on what your project entails and what you need/expect from each person. Communication is key throughout your project.
- Be professional. Show the local authority you're a professional investor, have done your research and are properly prepared.
- Use an 'umbrella' utility provider. It'll make your life so much easier.

DON'T

- Try to manage the whole project yourself. Instructing a lead contractor, who's on site every day and probably has his own team he's used to working with, is by far the most sensible option.
- Be afraid to ask for help and advice. Most local property professionals are happy to share their expertise.

Chapter 5

Preparing your schedule of works

This is your framework for the project. It's where the budget, jobs and materials are broken down and a timescale is applied. It's your roadmap, your bible, your blueprint for the work, so it needs to be accurate.

Because we've been in the business for many years, our schedule of works is a slick beast! We have a standard template that can very quickly be tweaked and tailored to each project, but the timeframe rarely changes and our contractors know they will usually need to work to a 4 to 7-week plan. Everything is standardised – our suppliers, our materials, fixtures, fittings, furnishings and décor – so we can budget and plan the work very quickly, as soon as we know what renovation and refurbishment the property requires.

But that's us and where we are now. How should you start?

Your initial scheme and scope of work

The first thing you need to do is have a template – we just use a Word document – that you can complete as you walk around the property, noting all the work that's going to need doing. Below is a same scheme for 'Property A', showing the categories we use, together with example notes, so you can get an idea of how the schedule starts:

Property A
Scheme outline
Currently:
- 3 bedroom terrace, 1960s
- Small front and back gardens
- Large living room and dining room connected
- Not in good decorative order

Convert to 5-bed HMO with 2 en-suites, 1 exclusive use of upstairs bathroom and 2 sharing downstairs bathroom (extended from current WC into utility room):
- Ground floor: Stud walls to separate living room and dining area. New bathroom for downstairs rooms to share.
- 1st Floor: 2 doubles to include new en-suites and smaller room given exclusive use of 1st floor bathroom.

Plan of work
Fire systems
- Full system – smoke detectors in all common parts and heat sensor in kitchen
- Emergency lighting above and below staircase
- Fire doors (7) closers and smoke baffle / intumescent strips

Internal walls
- Stud walls to separate existing living room and dining room

Kitchen

- Full refurbishment required

Plumbing

- En-suites created in two 1st floor bedrooms
- New bathroom downstairs into utility room
- Some work in existing bathroom (new shower, etc.)

Wiring

- Full rewiring required

TV distribution and digital aerial supply

- To all rooms

Re-keying

- Locks and keys to all doors to be refitted using master keying system.

Internal Decoration

- Full refurbishment of internal decoration required
- Furnishing and curtains for all bedrooms, as required

External

- No external issues
- Gardens easy care
- Parking locally is reasonable

Furnishings, curtains and lampshades

- Standard pack

Certification

- Gas safety certificate
- Electrical certificate
- HMO certificate not required in this case
- Fire alarm commissioning certificate

Once this information has been gathered, you can cost up the works to get an overall refurbishment budget.

Works budget

The first time you do this, it'll take some time to get quotes and estimates, but if you do a good job on that first project, you'll have all the figures to hand for the future. Here's an example of costs we allocated to the fairly comprehensive refurbishment of Property A:

Itemised Improvement Costs

Kitchen	£3,500
En-suites	£7,000
2 bathrooms (existing plus new)	£6,000
Boiler & megaflow hot water cylinder	£4,200
Fire safety works	£3,990
Rewiring	£3,500
Stud walls	£1,500
Mortgage payments during refurb	£2,500
Redecoration	£2,000
Recarpet	£2,500
Furnishing & curtains	£5,200
Rekeying	£950
Misc. labour	£1,200
Project management	£5,000
Contingency 5%	£2,500
Total	**£51,540**

Obviously, the costs above are a total relating to each job, which are broken down into much more detail elsewhere. As we said before, you can go into as much or as little detail as you like in your price research – you could itemise it down to each screw, but that might be taking it a bit far! However, as an example, 'Fire safety works' above would be made up of costs for:

- fire doors
- intumescent strips
- fire door closers
- smoke alarms
- heat sensors
- fire blanket (kitchen)
- extinguisher (kitchen)

As mentioned earlier, we let our contractors source their own materials, so the costs shown also include labour. When you first start out, you should certainly separate the two very clearly, so that you can see exactly how the costs are divided, but as you go on, you'll get to the point where you just know, for example, that an en-suite costs £3,500 (to include stud walls, tiling, all fixtures & fittings, plumbing material costs and labour). Just don't forget that, for tax purposes, the two need to be clearly separated.

Once you have your works budget and know the exact capital input required, you can go back to your viability analysis and check that the investment still stacks up and your ROI figure means it makes financial sense to proceed.

The final schedule of works

So you have a complete list of jobs and works, along with a budget for the project; now you need to look at the timescale. We've said that our team work to a 4 to 7-week timeframe as standard and that's a pretty good guide for you. If you don't have much work to do, you may be able to do everything in a month; in terms of it taking longer than 7 weeks, that shouldn't really happen. Two months plus is becoming a pretty serious renovation, probably involving structural work, and that's simply not the kind of property we'd recommend for a buy to let investment where you want to keep the timescale between completion and ready to rent as tight as you can.

While you don't need to know every last detail, you do need to make sure you get a full picture of what work is involved, the jobs that need to be carried out and the order in which everything needs to be done. So ask your project manager / lead builder to sit down with you and go through a typical HMO refurbishment. Make it clear you're not going to be hanging over his shoulder the whole way through, but it is important for you to know that by the end of week two, for example, X should be completed and work on X should be beginning.

It's also helpful – to you and your contractors – to have a rough floor plan, showing the existing layout and the changes you're planning to make. Virtually every property for sale these days has a floor plan, so you can simply copy that, and mark on it things like stud walls, new en-suites and bathrooms and other reconfigured rooms. For your first project, you will probably find a sketch of each room useful as well, where you can mark on where radiators and sockets will be and perhaps where the furniture will be situated. It's entirely up to you – do what makes you feel comfortable and able to best communicate exactly what you want and need from your team.

Here are some sample floor plans that we put together on PowerPoint:

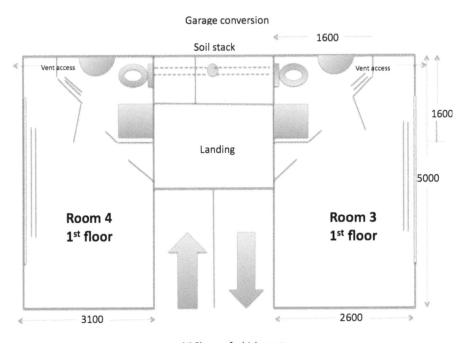

1st Floor refurbishment

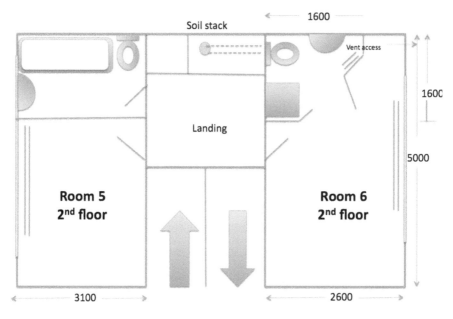

Soil stack

1600

Vent access

1600

5000

Room 5
2ⁿᵈ floor

Landing

Room 6
2ⁿᵈ floor

3100

2600

2ⁿᵈ Floor refurbishment

We said in the last chapter that problems can arise if one contractor starts blaming another's slow progress for not being able to get on with their next job and that's one of your project manager's main responsibilities: keeping everyone on schedule. And you can't assess whether he's doing his job properly if you don't know yourself what should be happening, so take some time to get it straight in your head and do a simple spreadsheet, broken down by days/weeks and jobs. If your tradespeople are very used to this kind of project, they should be pretty much bang on, but making it clear that you know more or less what they should be doing and when, means there's less chance of things slipping. Share this schedule with your team, get their feedback and make any tweaks, so you can be sure everyone's clear and on the same page right from the start.

We recently spoke to someone who'd had an absolute nightmare with her renovation project because she'd tried to manage everything herself, source all her own materials and had broken down every last cost. She'd spoken to her tradesmen in a huge amount of detail about the order in which they needed to do things and how long each task would take, and they really didn't understand why she needed to know. Her final spreadsheet of timescale and costs was so detailed it was virtually useless as a tool for effective management of the project, as none of the tradespeople could understand it! The project ended up overrunning because she managed to confuse her entire team, including herself; the materials she'd ordered never seemed to arrive at the right time and many of them were wrong; the team almost walked off the job because she was micro-managing to such an extent that it appeared she didn't trust them…it was probably the best example of why new investors shouldn't try to manage a whole project themselves!

Assuming you've chosen your contractors and tradespeople well, trust that they know what they're doing. Each of them has worked with other trades on projects numerous times and is used to communicating – plus, you have a lead contractor to project manage them for you - so don't bog yourself down with unnecessary detail.

We're all different in terms of the level of detail we're comfortable with, but you can waste a lot of time – as the lady in the example above did – concerning yourself with timescales and costs that really don't need to be broken down. On your first project, you'll undoubtedly find yourself wanting to do just that, because you want to know absolutely everything, but try to fight the urge!

Compile your information

You should now have everything you need to get started on your project. The software package we use condenses all the costs, budgets and analysis on the property and project into a PDF report that we send to our clients. That's obviously not something you necessarily need to do when it's your own project, but we'd advise you do something similar. That way, you have all your figures in one place for easy reference. You can download a FREE sample property report from nickfox.co.uk - here's a summary of what it contains:

- **Overview,** with purchase and mortgage figures, income and cash flow, plus KPIs
- **Full purchase analysis**, from which the Overview figures are taken, with capital input broken down, financial metrics, income and expenditure breakdown and various rate assumptions
- **Forward projections,** predicting income and expenditure for years 1-5, 10 and 25, plus scenarios for if you wanted to sell the property at various stages
- **Rent rates**
- **Itemised improvement costs** (as shown earlier in chapter)
- **Photographs of current condition.**

In terms of future projections, the report goes into quite some detail about loan rates, potential sale costs and values, and also includes graphs showing cash flow, anticipated market value and ROI. While you can use software packages to generate these figures, we'd recommend spending some time doing it yourself via spreadsheets, so that you really gain an understanding of how to calculate the way your project stacks up, both today and into the future. Once you understand that, you can move on to the short-cuts, if you wish – they certainly save time!

As far as all the background work for your analysis goes, Nick's first book, 'HMO PROPERTY SUCCESS', has lots of information on how to research rent rates, capital values, redecorating and furnishing costs, etc., so if you haven't already read it, you can buy a copy from nickfox.co.uk - and Nick will even sign it for you!

Finally, get yourself some storage

It's not quite 'works' but one thing it's a very good idea to do, particularly if you're intending to build a portfolio of several properties, is to organise some storage space. During works, things may be delivered before the property is actually ready to accommodate them, such as bathroom suites, kitchens or furniture, and you're going to have to house them somewhere.

So look into renting a garage or other similar unit (which is usually cheaper than a storage unit with Safestore, Big Yellow, etc.) and build that into your budget. It'll be really useful, not only during renovation and refurbishment, but also as your tenants change. Some people want to bring their own bed and some have property they'd like to store safely while they're with you – there are lots of situations where, as a landlord, having a decent storage space makes your life a lot easier – and you may be able to charge tenants a little extra as well.

DO

- Take lots of photographs. Check with the vendor/agent that it's okay, but there shouldn't be any problem. It's amazing what you forget once you leave a property.
- Get hold of a floorplan. It doesn't have to be to scale, but you need to be clear on what's where and on the way you're planning to divide the space.
- Check and double-check your figures. Do your research well and keep an eye on your KPIs.
- Take advice from your contractors. They'll have some reliable, cost-effective recommendations for you.
- Secure some storage space. Garages are ideal, but make sure they're watertight.

DON'T

- Bog yourself down with too many details. You need to know how much the project's going to cost, but you don't need to know the price of every pot of paint and exactly how long it'll take the plumber to fit the WC!
- Try to source all the materials yourself. Let your contractors get their own supplies and fittings where you can.
- Rush. Take time to put together your schedules and budgets – the success of the project relies heavily on the planning.

PART TWO:

THE PROJECT

Chapter 6

So you've found a property...

...let's have a re-cap. By the time you've found what you think could be a great investment, you should:

Know:
- you can do this!
- all your project costs
- that your investment stacks up
- your KPIs: profit, ROI, yield
- how long the project's going to take
- all the legal and local council requirements you must comply with.

Have:
- your finances in place
- your team in place
- a full viability analysis spreadsheet
- a schedule of works that your team has approved and understands
- the foundations for a good on-going relationship with your local council officers.

If there's anything you're not clear on at this stage, or you're struggling to get hold of the right advisors or tradespeople, email us at hello@nickfox.co.uk and we'll do our best to help you.

Before you make your formal offer, go back and 'stress-test' your figures. Consult with your builder and make sure you haven't missed anything off the main budget. Even though you will be having a survey, take your builder / lead contractor around with you when you view the property for a second time. You will have spotted certain things yourself, but, assuming your builder is experienced in converting HMOs, he'll be able to advise you about potential issues, spot any problems with the fabric of the property and will probably bring up things that you might not have considered, good and bad.

When you make your offer, make sure you put it in writing and if it's below the asking price, briefly outline your reasons for settling on that value. Confirm your position, reassure them that everything's in place in terms of legals and financials, and state the suggested timescale for exchange and completion, along with any other terms you may have already discussed, such as furnishings being included. The more prepared and professional you can show yourself to be, the more likely the agent is to support you as a buyer.

Timetable, from offer to completion

The clock starts ticking from the moment your offer is accepted and the solicitors are instructed.

If you're not already familiar with the conveyancing procedure, a guide is on the next page (process and timescale may vary slightly). A standard house purchase, where a chain is involved, takes around 3 months, although you may be able to negotiate to aim for less. This is where the importance of having a good solicitor / conveyancer comes in – they can really help move the process along. But, no matter how good your legal representative is, you should still be familiar with the process, so that you know what questions to ask of both your solicitor and the agent. Again, it comes down to being informed and looking knowledgeable and professional.

Purchase	Sale
Instruct your solicitor. Compete and return their instruction paperwork - including proof of identity documents - and forward a cheque to cover their initial costs, as requested (usually c.£100).	

Estate agent sends sales particulars to all parties.

	Vendor's solicitor prepares the contract pack and sends it to your solicitor.

Contract pack is received. Your solicitor aplies for Searches, checks the Title documents and raises any enquiries with the vendor's solicitor.

	Vendor's solicitor responds to enquiries.

Once your solicitor has received replies to enquiries, results of Searches and your mortgage offer, they will report to you on the Title and arrange for you to sign the contract. You should arrange for your deposit to be forwarded to your solicitor, in readiness for exchange.

Both parties sign contracts.

Your solicitor confirms receipt of deposit funds.

Completion date is agreed.

Contracts are exchanged.

A completion statement is sent to you, detailing the balance required to complete (including Stamp Duty Land Tax and all other costs associated with the purchase). This must be settled with your solicitor before completion.

Your solicitor orders mortgage funds from the lender.

On the completion date, your solicitor transfers funds to the vendor's solicitor, pays the SDLT to HMRC and applies to the Land Registry to register you as the new owner.

	Vendor's solicitor confirms receipt of funds and instructs the estate agent to release the keys to you.

While the purchase is going through…

Assuming you haven't been able to gain early access to the property to begin any works – which is the case most of the time, as people are usually still living there! – this is the time when you should be getting everything in order to enable you to hit the ground running as soon as you complete.

Have a good walk-through of the property

This is to enable you to complete your draft schedule of works. Your builder may already have given you all the advice you need on the second viewing, but you should have him come on this visit with you, which should take around an hour and a half. This is when you should note everything pertinent to the project, such as:

- confirming the layout & stud walls required
- details of any garage or loft conversions
- noting refits of kitchen and bathrooms
- condition of boiler
- locations of additional en-suites and other plumbing
- condition of electrics and additional sockets etc. that may be required
- number of fire doors required
- condition of décor
- parking arrangements
- general condition of fabric of property & where refurb to that will be required
- external examination

This will give you an idea of what the surveyor might report, but your builder will be able to give you an idea of costs there and then for any significant problems so you can plan any renegotiation that may be necessary. Note: It's not good practice to renegotiate the price after the sale has been agreed, but sometimes, if a significant extra cost comes to light through closer inspection, backed up by the surveyor's report, it's justified.

Confirm details with local council

Contact the relevant people you spoke to when carrying out your research, tell them that you have a purchase underway and check everything is as you understood it to be. If it turns out that something major now stands in the way – such as it being unlikely that permission for an HMO would be granted – you're still at the stage where you could pull out of the purchase, if necessary.

Firm up terms of engagement with contractors

We've worked with the same team for a long time and have a relationship where neither party feels the need for a formal, signed agreement, but for your first project with a new team, it's not a bad idea to have a 'Terms of Engagement' in writing, to include the following:

- names of both parties
- state what the job is
- confirm the timescale
- payment details (we'd recommend 40% deposit up front, stage payments and a 12% snagging retention)
- signed by both parties.

As we said earlier, one of the key elements in the success of your project is a clear line of communication with your team. Putting everything in writing ensures there won't be any debate later on about who said what. Attach it to the job quote that you've accepted from each tradesperson and file it safely.

Select fixtures, fittings and furnishings

You'll already have done your research and got quotes and prices; now's the time to firm up on everything and get it ordered. Double-check with your contractors that they're supplying everything you think they are – you don't want your plumber asking you on week three of the project when the bathroom suite's arriving, if you presumed he was ordering it!

Get your deposit funds ready

That might sound obvious, but it's amazing the number of people who forget their capital is in a savings account with restrictions on withdrawal, or who think they can give their solicitor a cheque on the day of exchange. Find out from your solicitor / conveyancer when they would like to be in receipt of the funds and make sure you allow time for electronic transfers or cheques to be cashed.

Get your works funding organised

We recommend you pay your contractors 40% up front, then make stage payments, plus there will be outlay for the fixtures, fittings and furnishings you're buying yourself, so just go back through your schedule and make sure you have money in the right places.

It's worth having another conversation with your tax advisor and/or IFA to make sure you understand the most beneficial and tax-efficient way to pay for everything.

After exchange – conversations with people

Again, we can't stress enough the importance of communication during this process, so once you have a firm completion date:

Liaise with your project manager

Confirm the team is committed to being on site from day one. Go back though your schedule of works with your project manager and make sure everything's in hand. One thing in particular he may ask you to do is book a skip, so remember to ask the question.

Apply for planning permissions, if necessary, and notify the council of when the building works will begin

We get the HMO Officer and Building Control out to the property as soon as possible after completion, so now is the time to make an appointment with them.

Contact your utility provider/s

Let them know you've exchanged, discuss the works timescale and find out what notice they need to make sure everything's live when it needs to be.

Speak to your insurer

You'll now be able to give them firm dates for work starting. Be absolutely clear on what they require you to inform them about, to make sure you're always properly covered.

Inform the neighbours

As soon as you've exchanged and have a start date for your works, let the neighbours know what's going to be happening. It's not only a matter of courtesy to warn them about potential disruption, but you also want to build good relationships with the people who will actually be your tenants' neighbours. Knock on their door to introduce yourself, so they can see you're not just another 'faceless' landlord, let them know you're happy to talk through any concerns they might have, and ask them to contact you right away if there are any problems.

DO

- Stress-test your figures before you make an offer. Do all you can at this stage to reduce the possibility of having to revise or withdraw your offer once the sale has been agreed.

- Put your offer in writing, clearly setting out your proposed terms and position.

- Make sure you understand the purchase process. That way, you can monitor how things are progressing.

- Keep referring to your schedule. The first time you do a project like this, it'll seem as though there's an enormous number of plates to keep spinning. There are a lot, but as long as you've prepared properly and got it all written down, you'll be fine!

- Keep speaking to people. Your project manager, council officers, other local property professionals...they're all here to help you. Don't be a pest, but don't be afraid to ask for advice when you need it. They'll all understand that your first project can seem quite a hurdle.

DON'T

- Forget to get your capital ready! Check with your solicitor when your deposit need to be transferred and confirm your contractors' payment schedule with your project manager.

Chapter 7

It's yours: work begins

We're repeating what we said in Chapter 2, but the tax issue is well worth bringing up again at this point. This project is, first and foremost, a financial investment and 'revenue' versus 'capital' is a division of investment and expenditure that you must be clear on before any money goes out.

Have your tax advisor give you some guidelines on how to ensure that as much of your renovation and refurbishment outgoings as possible can be allocated as revenue: that's one of the biggest tricks in terms of making this project as financially beneficial to you as it can be. Revenue items (expenditure related to operating the business of buy to let) are tax-deductible; capital items (things that improve the value of the property) can only be deducted against capital gains when you sell the property. We're not going to go into any particular detail here, and would emphasise that we're not qualified to give advice, but make sure you have this specific conversation with your advisor.

It's also a conversation you should have with your contractors, because they'll need to be very clear on their invoices with breakdowns that enable your tax advisor to prove to HMRC what's been spent where.

Now, putting HMRC to one side, let's get the renovation and refurbishment underway!

The team gets stuck in

Before you let anyone over the threshold to start work, you must ensure you have the appropriate indemnity insurance in place, to cover you for any accidents or injuries on site. Phone your insurer, explain exactly what works are about to take place and make sure you're properly protected.

The first couple of days of the project are likely to be mainly skip filling, as walls are stripped, dated fittings are ripped out and the property is cleared ready for the new works to begin.

Start off the project by having a meeting with the team just to check everyone's clear, happy and there aren't any unexpected problems. Most tradespeople on projects like this bring their own flasks and food, etc., but it's nice if you can provide some refreshments for them – electrics and water permitting! Put a kettle and some mugs on a tray, along with tea, coffee, sugar, some UHT milk and biscuits. A fed and watered team is a happy team!

Bring in the HMO Officer and Building Control

You should already have made appointments for the HMO / Amenity Standards Officer and Building Control Officer to come on site as early as possible. Go over again exactly what you're doing and if either of them raise any issues, try to resolve them there and then. This is the stage where it's not too late to change where you put stud walls and tweak any other parts of the plan.

Building Control may need to make stage visits to sign off work, so make sure you're clear on when those are required. Also ask the HMO Officer to come back when the work's almost complete, just to make sure before you send the contractors away that there's nothing else you need to do to be compliant. If the HMO Officer isn't able to help you with fire safety and a risk assessment, you should also ask the local Fire Safety Officer to visit.

Keeping on top of the schedule

As we've already said, the clearer your schedule of works, the easier it'll be to keep on top of things. With your first project, you'll probably want to spend quite a lot of time on site, so you can see how everything is done and watch the HMO coming together; just make sure you're not getting in the way!

We tend to make weekly visits and do a 'checkpoint report' for our clients every Friday, which ensures everything's on track. It details where we're up to, what's happened this week, what's happening next week and any issues that have come up. We also include pictures of the work.

It's so important to take notes and photographs all the way along. Not only is it good to have as evidence of what's happened when and the quality of work, but it'll also help you in knowing what to watch out for and what you can refine in your next project. Also, you may only be concerned with your own HMO projects right now, but you may decide a few years down the line (as we did) that you'd like to expand your business, and you'll have a well-documented portfolio of work ready to show. You may also need or want to go into a joint venture with a partner in the future – again, you'll have evidence of your project work already prepared.

Here are some photographs charting the progress of an en-suite bathroom:

And, just from a quirky aspect, we often put up pictures of the different stages of work in the hallways of our properties, as a fun and interesting talking point!

Keep an eye on the quality of work as it progresses, essentially snagging as you go along. It's much easier to put faults right as they happen, rather than waiting until the whole house is finished. Also, it helps the contractors to be clear on the standard you expect and snagging is something they expect you, as the client, to do.

If there are any big problems and you're not happy with any aspect of the work itself, the site or the tradespeople, talk to your project manager and ask him to help you resolve them. A lead builder has carpenters, plumbers, etc. that work for him, so he should be your first port of call with any concerns.

We once had a decorator whose work was just awful. He was part of our lead contractor's recommended team, so we told him we weren't happy with the quality and suggested he replace the decorator himself, or else we would have to. He agreed and found someone else whose work was much better. It's all about setting expectations, being clear on the quality you demand and trusting your instincts if you get a gut feeling something's not right. Address issues right away – don't bury your head in the sand and then complain at the end that things are wrong. As we said right at the start, you have to be good at managing people and not afraid to stand your ground if you're not happy with something or someone. Just remember that a happy worker is a good worker, so here are our top tips for keeping your team upbeat:

1) Make sure they feel valued and appreciated. When they're doing a good job, tell them they're doing a good job.

2) Have a sense of humour – keep the atmosphere light and positive.

3) Communicate well with them. If they're not doing something as you'd like it done, tell them nicely as soon as you spot it – they should appreciate you being honest and up front.

4) Be on site. Take a real interest and show them that their work and a good atmosphere on site matters to you.

5) Be considerate. Before we visit the property, we tend to pop to the shops and arrive with sandwiches, biscuits and some drinks.

A tale of warning

If, regardless of everything we've said so far, you're tempted to cut corners and throw yourself in at the deep end, here's a case study that we hope will put you off!

Last year we sourced a property for a lady who decided she didn't want our refurbishment service and could handle it all herself. She brought in a team of eastern European builders, who didn't understand the building regulations in this country, and didn't involve either Building Control or the HMO Officer. When she asked us to go in and do an audit for her, as she lived some distance away, we actually found a couple of the builders sleeping, and what should have taken 7-8 weeks ended up taking almost twice as long.

We don't believe the work was done correctly and it certainly wasn't finished off to standard. She won't have any warranties for the work and not only runs the risk of getting a knock on the door from the local authority, but is also likely to be letting unsafe accommodation, opening her tenants up to danger and herself up to fines and prosecution if anything should go wrong in the property.

Our original research and analysis showed she should have been able to charge £500-600 per room but we later saw the property advertised at £300-£400 per room. While she thought she was saving money by not paying us, it was a complete false economy and she won't be achieving anywhere near the returns she could have.

If you're going to use a letting agent...

...or have a private property manager, bring them in early on. Let them see the property and listen to any thoughts they have on what tenants really love or hate and what things you might need to therefore tweak in your plans. If this is the person who's going to be letting your properties on your behalf, give them a reason to be enthusiastic about the home they're 'selling' to tenants and make them feel they've had a hand in creating desirable accommodation.

Marketing the rooms/property

Ideally, you want to have tenants lined up and ready to move into the property as soon as the refurbishment is finished, so you should start marketing as soon as the site is safe enough for people to walk around. (Double-check that your indemnity insurance is watertight first!). From a health & safety point of view, when taking people into the property, you must make sure you clearly state that work is currently being done and point out any particular things that might pose a danger, such as dustsheets on the floor, loose boards and electrical leads from equipment.

If this is your first project, you won't yet have any photos of what the finished property is likely to look like, but you can take external shots and have floor plan sketches and pictures of the furnishings from your suppliers, to give prospective tenants an idea. We always find that, rather than people being put off by not being able to see the end result, they're keen to secure a room in a freshly-renovated property, where everything's new.

Again, our book 'HMO PROPERTY SUCCESS' has more information about advertising and marketing so grab yourself a copy now from nickfox.co.uk or Amazon.co.uk. You can also order the audiobook from Audible.co.uk or iTunes. Kindle and iBook versions are also available.

DO

- Have another conversation with your tax advisor. Make sure you've correctly understood their advice.
- Get the council officers in asap. You don't want to have to undo work and throw your schedule out.
- Make sure your team's happy!
- Snag as you go along, and communicate with your project manager if anything's not up to standard.
- Take lots of notes and photos as work progresses.
- Begin to market the property early. You need rent to start coming in as soon as possible.

DON'T

- Cut corners. Carry out proper research, exercise due diligence and make sure you always use the right contractors, suppliers and materials for each job.
- Leave snagging to the end. It's much easier to fix problems as they arise.

Chapter 8

Fixtures, fittings and furnishings

If you're not strict with yourself, this is where you can spend way too much money for little or no gain in revenue. This is not your own home, it's a business and, while you need a good finish, you don't need the absolute highest quality.

And no matter how objective you think you are, there are a lot of people who find it hard to rein things in and stick to a strict scheme and budget when it comes to a newly acquired property. So if you find yourself tempted to push the boat out a bit, you're not alone! We actually had one client who wanted to use Farrow & Ball paint in the HMO we were refurbishing for them, because they thought the colour was nicer than the standard, hard-wearing, always-available, neutral paint we use in all our properties! That's an extreme example, but we do find that – certainly on their first project – new investors tend to want to make each property and each room within the property individual.

There's nothing wrong with the sentiment, but if you go down that road you often end up with rooms that aren't gender-neutral enough and with lots of extra accessories that tenants either disregard or damage.

Just to prove that it happens to us all, Richard will confess to having asked someone to hand-make all the curtains for his first HMO! Needless to say, he only did it that once and now gets them from Dunelm, the very reasonably-priced curtain specialist...

What tenants want

Tenants want a decent-sized bedroom that they can make their own, solid comfortable furniture, spacious communal areas and a well-equipped kitchen that's easy to keep looking clean and tidy. That's it. They're not bothered about pretty curtains, a room that's different to their neighbour's or having a wrought-iron bedstead. You can have lovely curtains made to measure for £2-3,000, or buy a similar look off the rack at a quarter of the price. As long as they close, keep the light out and the heat in, the tenant's happy – and so is your ROI.

Tenants renting rooms tend to have a 6-9 month tenure, so you're looking at an average of 3-4 changeovers every two years; that could easily be 24 different people moving through the property in that time – plus each of them has friends, bikes, boxes being lugged in and out. In short, there's quite a lot of wear and tear on an HMO. And, while it's broadly true that the more you pay, the longer something lasts, that's not what you want in an HMO. You want to be able to keep it looking fresh and know that the price you're paying for furnishings and décor is at a level where you're happy to replace items more frequently than you would ever think of doing in your own home.

That being said, don't be tempted to go for the cheapest option. Cheap flat-pack falls apart if it's moved even once and, as we've discovered, tenants often like to shift things about in their rooms. Cheap fittings, such as toilet-roll holders and kitchen taps, quickly become loose and fall apart. Your contractors, and especially the ones who you'll retain to carry out on-going maintenance, will have experience of things failing and should be able to guide you to a happy middle ground.

Develop a standard theme

The only things that really change from one HMO to another are the layout and number of rooms, and those things make absolutely no difference to the fixtures, fittings & furnishings, other than the quantity you require. So when you're selecting the 'look' for your first project, make sure you choose things that tend to be mass-manufactured and will be available for the foreseeable future. Do your shopping list properly once and it'll make life so much easier the second, third and fourth time…

There are several good reasons for using the same supplies and suppliers time and again:

- It gives you a brand and therefore a consistency of standard and appeal across all your properties, making advertising so much easier
- You can often negotiate discounts for bulk-buying
- You know you'll be able to replace an item quickly and easily when you need to

- If your scheme is standard, it makes budgeting quicker and project managing less stressful.

We go to suppliers that are national and have a reputation for producing decent products at very reasonable prices. We're not going to go through our entire inventory here, but to give you an idea:

- We get our beds from Mr Mattress, the mattress specialist, and they're just simple divans with storage underneath - lightweight, easy to move in and out and not expensive.
- Our headboards we source from a supplier on eBay. They're just padded pieces that slide onto rails on the walls and then we push the divans up against them. They're £50 and look great.
- Wardrobes, drawers and bedside cabinets are from IKEA – flat pack, easy to put together and really solid.
- Curtains are simple ring-tops from Dunelm, the curtain specialist.
- Paint is trade Dulux or similar – easy to find in a number of outlets, meaning our maintenance team can use the same pot for touch-ups across the entire portfolio.

For carpets, you should be able to find a good local fitter who'll do an entire HMO for around £2,000, including underlay. The important thing to ensure is that it's a common product and cost-effective, i.e. hard wearing but not expensive to replace, as stained and damaged carpets are a real turn-off for tenants.

In terms of kitchen and bathroom fittings, tiles, fixtures, etc., your contractors should be able to source those for you. Bathroom suites need to be simple, white and chrome, so they look hygienic, are easy to clean and each element is easy to replace. Your kitchen should be neutral with white or chrome/silver appliances, and we find a dark grey tiled floor is hard wearing, easy to keep clean and ages well.

We referred to this earlier in the chapter, but it really is important to make the scheme gender-neutral. Keeping everything simple should mean it's equally appealing to male and female tenants.

Here are some pictures from our portfolio, so you can see the kind of finish you're looking to achieve:

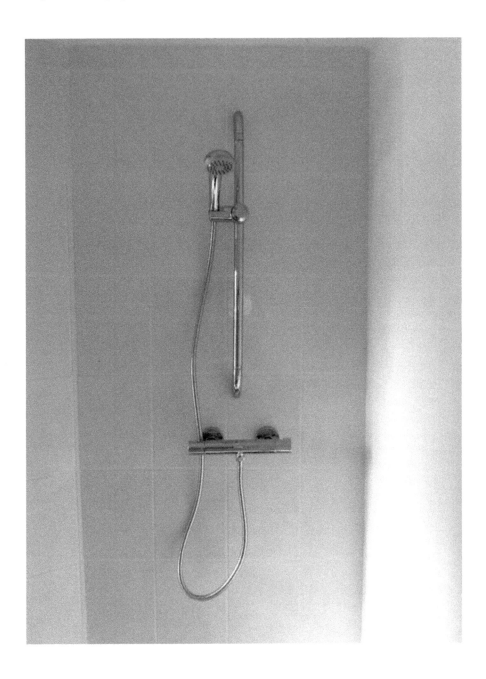

I've seen a number of properties that landlords have done to a higher spec, that are really impressive, but those tend to be in and around Central London, where people can afford to pay for and expect the very best, even in a shared house. For the vast majority of us, investing outside London, the finish we recommend is just the right balance: it looks clean, smart and modern, but (1) it's in proportion to the rent people can afford to pay, at the higher end of the scale, and (2) it fits with the ROI and monthly profit figures we look for. And those are the only two things that you need to concern yourself with.

What furniture & furnishings do I need?

We provide the following as standard in our HMOs:

Bedrooms:
- Divan bed (double or single, as required) plus headboard
- Chest of drawers
- Wardrobe
- A single bedside table
- Curtains

Kitchens:
- Double oven with 4-ring hob
- One fridge shelf and one freezer drawer per tenant – normally two fridges per property
- Washing machine
- Tumble dryer

- Microwave
- Kettle
- Vacuum cleaner
- Mop & bucket
- Clothes dryer
- Toaster

Communal area/s:
- Dining table and seating for minimum 4 people
- Curtains
- Sofa & chairs, if area permits
- Information board

Do bear in mind that if you provide lamps in bedrooms, they will have to be tested by an electrician every year, as do all other portable electrical appliances in the house (PAT). While this is easy for kitchen appliances, it may be harder to arrange access to a tenant's room and if the lamp is untested, your insurance is unlikely to cover you if it causes damage or harm to the tenant.

Keys

Over the years, we've seen and tried a number of different lock and key systems – round handles with the keyhole in the middle, auto-closing Yale locks, keypads – but by far the best, and the one we use in every property now is the master key system, also knows as 'suited' keys. Each tenant has a key that only opens the main front door and their door, while you, the maintenance team and property manager can hold a single key that accesses every room in the property. If you set up the system in the right way when you refurbish your first property, you can have a master that opens every door in every property.

It really is a great system, which you only really appreciate when you have multiple properties. Under the old system we used, where every door had its own lock and key, we had to hold a large bunch for each house. The master suited system cuts down on the time you and your maintenance team have to spend looking for keys and makes organising storage much simpler.

At £800-£900 per property, it's more expensive than having a Chubb or Yale single-key system, but it really does pay for itself time and time again. Any good master locksmith should be able to provide this for you.

DO

- Keep uppermost in your mind that this is a business. Think about your target tenant and what they want – don't be tempted to overspend for the sake of 'prettying it up'.
- Focus on a theme/scheme you can easily replicate. Source from major suppliers or local providers of good-quality basics.
- Always try to negotiate discounts for bulk buying.
- Look into getting a master suited key system.

DON'T

- Over-decorate. You'll spend more than you need to and complicate the on-going maintenance.
- Buy the cheapest option. Nine times out of ten, that's a false economy. You want cost-effective, not cheap.

Chapter 9

Tying up the project

As the renovation and refurbishment comes to an end, it's a good idea to put together a checklist to make sure you've covered everything off, in terms of the works, your legal responsibilities and making sure the property is safe, warm and ready for tenants to move in.

Snagging

Although you will have been snagging periodically throughout the project, if you don't check thoroughly that all the work has been finished off to your satisfaction and address any problems at this stage, while the contractors are still on site, things can get painful. Having to go back at a later date can cause bad feeling, delays in problems being rectified (as tradespeople are likely to be on other jobs) and potentially delay tenants moving in.

You should have agreed up front that there would be a 12% retention on the contractors' invoices until you're happy with all the work, so your team will be expecting this final snagging. Go through each room in the property, preferably with your project manager, checking that all the following is up to the standard you expect:

Bedrooms:

- Paintwork – walls, ceiling, skirting and coving all neat
- Carpet – properly fitted and finished off at edges and doorways
- Curtains – poles straight and secure at correct height
- Blinds – working properly and secure
- Light fittings – in the right place and at correct height
- Light switches – straight and operating the correct light
- Sockets – sufficient and straight
- Radiators – straight and working properly

Bathrooms:

- Paintwork – neat & correct finish
- Tiling – straight and grouting properly finished
- WC, bath, shower unit & basin – secure and edges properly sealed
- Shower & bath – work properly
- Taps, hooks & holders – secure
- Correct light fitting
- Correct ventilation
- Heated towel rail working

Kitchen:

- Paintwork – neat & correct finish
- Tiling – straight and grouting properly finished
- Flooring – solid and properly finished off at the edges & doorways

- Units – secure & all doors and drawers functioning well
- Sink – draining properly and taps secure and working well
- Cooker & white goods - all connected and working properly
- Correct light fitting
- Correct ventilation
- Light fittings – in the right place and at correct height
- Light switches – straight and operating the correct light
- Sockets – sufficient and straight
- Radiators – straight and working properly
- Blinds – working properly and secure

Other communal areas:
- Paintwork – walls, ceiling, skirting and coving all neat
- Carpet – properly fitted and finished off at edges and doorways
- Curtains – poles straight and secure at correct height
- Blinds – working properly and secure
- Light fittings – in the right place and at correct height
- Light switches – straight and operating the correct light
- Sockets – sufficient and straight
- Radiators – straight and working properly

Make a list of any problems and have your project manager liaise with the relevant tradespeople to remedy them. Then do what will, hopefully, be a final check, confirm you're happy and have each trade issue you with a warranty for the work they've done. We expect all our contractors to give us an absolute minimum of a 6-month warranty and most are happy to guarantee their work for 12 months. Once you have those warranties, make sure you pay the contractors the balance of what you owe them as soon as possible.

Your maintenance team

Don't forget to thank your contractors and tell them how much you appreciate their hard work. You're going to need them again in the future and this is the time when you want to firm up on your on-going maintenance team. While a general handyman is the person you'll be calling on most often, you do need a plumber who is happy to come out quickly when needed, and an electrician who also won't take an age to fix problems. One of the reasons it's so important to build up a good rapport with them during the works and pay them on time is that you want them to put you to the top of the list when you need something doing.

Although you do need to keep a careful record of who holds what keys and don't want to have too many floating about, we find the easiest thing is if we give both our plumber and our electrician master keys, in addition to the handyman and cleaner. If they're good, they'll have a steady flow of work and are unlikely to be able to give you exact times when they'll be able to pop to your property between other bigger jobs. You want problems fixed quickly and if they don't have a key, it can be a real pain for your property manager – or you – to have to drop everything and rush to meet them or, worse, keep missing them so that problems drag on.

Once the contractors have finished all their work, get a cleaner in to do a thorough post-build clean (be sure to tell them that's what the job is!) to make sure the place is sparkling. And before you pay them, as with the other contractors' work, check you're happy that they've done a good job and there's no trace of building dust, etc.

Certification

In addition to guarantees and warranties for the work, you need to ensure you have the following valid certificates before you can legally let the property:

Gas Safety Certificate. This should be provided by the engineer (Gas Safe registered) who installed or serviced your boiler. It's something that needs to be done annually, so make sure both you and the engineer have diarised when it's due for renewal.

An Electrical Installation Condition Report Certificate. All fixed electrical installations must be inspected and tested by a 'Part P'-qualified electrician at least every five years. Even if your HMO falls outside licensing regulations, the local authority can still ask to see a valid certificate within seven days. So do make sure you get this from your electrician before he leaves the property.

Both these certificates should be clearly displayed in the property – we'd suggest the best place is on a nicely-fitted notice board in the kitchen.

Fire Alarm Commissioning Certificate. After the alarm system has been installed by an appropriately qualified engineer, you will be issued with this certificate, which the local council will need to see.

And, although it's not currently legally required in an HMO, where tenants are sharing facilities, make sure you file the property's **Energy Performance Certificate (EPC).** If you ever let the property as a single unit or decide to sell, you'll need it. When you bought the property, the EPC would have formed part of the documentation and it's valid for 10 years; however, if you've improved the energy efficiency, with insulation or upgrading the glazing, it's worth getting the property re-inspected to try and raise the rating.

Get your local council officers back again

This visit shouldn't throw up any issues, provided you've had the HMO Officer and Building Control out to the property previously and taken their advice, as we recommend. This time, you're just asking them to confirm that they're happy everything's been done to standard. Ask the HMO Officer to confirm in writing that the property has been registered with them and that you've complied to all amenity and fire standards. If you require one, they will issue you with a 5-year licence. The Building Control team will confirm that you've carried out all the work under a building notice and will issue you with a completion certificate.

You also need to have an appropriate person carry out your Fire Safety Risk Assessment. The HMO Officer might be able to do it for you; if not, speak to your local Fire Safety Officer or the Fire Protection Association (FPA) to make an appointment. You may have to pay somewhere in the region of £150 to £300 but that's very little for the peace of mind it offers.

Contact suppliers

You should have already spoken to your insurance and utility providers, but get back in touch with them to make sure everything's in order and you're connected and covered as you think you should be. Make sure you've registered with the council for Council Tax and that they're aware of when the property is changing from empty to occupied.

Take advertising photos before tenants move in

Although you'll be letting the rooms furnished but without linen and bedding, you should still 'dress' the rooms to take some photographs. This is where you're allowed to indulge your interior design urges! Make up the beds (you can use the same furnishings for each room that you're photographing), put some cushions and throws on them, plug in a couple of lamps and get artistic with your lens.

Similarly, put a bowl of fruit in the kitchen, a plant and towels in the bathroom, flowers on the dining table, etc. Add some colour to your neutral scheme and make the place look really inviting. And understand that it will never again look as good as it does now! If you're tempted to leave any of your dressing items, we'd recommend you don't. Vases will get broken, plants will be left to die…and so on. Remember that this is a communal house and the tenants probably won't know each other, so there's very little sense of responsibility for anything in the communal areas. As we've said before, just make sure they're clean, functional and easy to keep that way.

Make an information file for the property

A great way to welcome new tenants is with a file containing useful property information, primarily relating to health and safety. We'd suggest it contains:

- Contact details for the property manager
- Details of what to do and who to contact in an emergency
- Copies of instruction manuals for appliances
- Copies of the gas and electrical safety certificates, plus EPC
- Broadband WiFi password / connection details

Some people also include local taxi numbers, take-away menus and bus routes – it's entirely up to you. The most important contact and fire safety information should also be displayed clearly on your kitchen notice board.

And don't put any original documents in the file, as things tend to go walkabout. The best way to prepare it is to scan all the documents into an electronic file, so that you can easily print out copies if anything is missing.

Organise your own office

As we said in Chapter 1, this business demands that you're organised. Make sure you've got everything filed and noted in a way that makes sense to you. As your portfolio grows, you'll need to be able to lay your hands on the right documentation relating to the right property very easily, so take your time and make sure you're recording things properly.

A very important thing for you to keep on top of is renewal dates for certificates and licences. Many of the suppliers and service providers will contact you in good time themselves to remind you, but you need to set up some kind of alert system for:

- Annual gas safety check
- Annual PAT
- 5-yearly electrical installation check
- Annual TV licence renewal
- Annual property insurance renewal

Whoever is managing the property should also be carrying out regular fire alarm testing (we carry this out every 2 weeks) and arranging quarterly periodical room inspections.

Keep all your receipts from the refurbishment and furnishing and file them separately from the expenditure you'll have for future maintenance. We'd actually recommend you engage a bookkeeper to keep track of your income and expenditure on an on-going basis - your tax advisor will be able to point you in the direction of someone who's familiar with bookkeeping for HMO investors.

Thank the neighbours

Importantly, knock on the neighbours' doors to let them know the work is finished, thank them for their patience and understanding while the project's been going on. Let them have your or your property manager's details in case there are any problems with tenants in the future.

Be sure they understand that the property is an HMO and that there will be multiple tenants coming and going, but reassure them that the tenants will all be working adults, carefully screened, and that the HMO is permitted and approved by the council.

And that's it - you've completed your first HMO renovation and refurbishment project! If you've followed all our advice, you should now be the proud owner of a high quality, legally compliant, desirable room-rental residence that's been approved by the local authority. And as long as your research and budgeting was done properly and the project was successfully managed, you can be confident that the rental income will start coming in to give you the returns you want and deserve.

This is only the first step on the HMO journey – how you manage your buy to let business into the future will ultimately determine your success, but as long as you continue to be diligent and build relationships with the people who can help you stay on top of the game, there's no reason why you shouldn't build a profitable and enviable portfolio.

Now, on to the next project…!

Checklist

- ☐ First round of snagging completed
- ☐ HMO Officer confirmed everything's up to standard and the property has been registered with the council
- ☐ Fire Safety Risk Assessment completed
- ☐ Building Control sign-off
- ☐ Gas & electrical safety certificates obtained and displayed
- ☐ Fire Alarm Commissioning Certificate obtained and presented to council
- ☐ Warranties and guarantees for all the work obtained
- ☐ Warranties and guarantees for all appliances registered
- ☐ Second snagging completed to satisfaction
- ☐ Balance of snagging retainer (12%) paid to contractor
- ☐ Full commercial clean of property
- ☐ Rooms dressed and photographs taken
- ☐ Neighbours thanked
- ☐ Correct number of keys in hand
- ☐ Cleaner engaged for on-going cleaning of communal areas & key given
- ☐ Handyman (or similar) engaged for maintenance & key given
- ☐ Plumber and electrician given keys
- ☐ Gardener engaged
- ☐ Council tax, TV licence and utilities all in order
- ☐ Information file left in the property
- ☐ Administration procedures set up

Ready to apply what you've learned?

Great! Here's even more from Nick Fox Property Mentoring

Thanks for taking the time to read this book - hopefully you've found it helpful and are inspired to put some or all of it into practice!

If you'd like to extend your knowledge, the next step is to check out our website, where you'll find lots of free information and details of our mentoring packages.

We offer a range of options to suit all needs, from short intensive taster sessions to more comprehensive packages that will give you a deeper understanding of property investment and the buy to let market, focusing on the rewards and implications of building an HMO portfolio:

- Half-day 'HMO Education and Tour'
- One-day 'Intensive HMO Property Mentoring Course'
- Two-day 'Intensive HMO Property Mentoring Course'
- 12 months' full access to and support from Nick Fox and his Power Team

Whichever package you choose, you can be assured that Nick's commitment to your personal property goals are absolute. Nick and his team get a real kick out of watching others grow their property portfolios by helping them implement the most successful methods that have been tried and tested over many years.

As skilled and experienced professionals, we present our mentoring sessions in such a way that they're easy to understand, while enabling highly effective learning. The acute insights and practical methodology on offer will help you to take your property business to the next level and secure financial independence for you and your loved ones.

Check out our website **nickfox.co.uk** or call us on **01908 930369** to find out more.

Find us on
FACEBOOK Nick Fox Mentor
TWITTER NickFoxPropertyMentoring
EMAIL hello@nickfox.co.uk
TEL 01908 930369

NICK FOX PROPERTY MENTORING
Suite 150, MK Business Centre, Foxhunter Drive,
Linford Wood, Milton Keynes MK14 6BL

Write a review and get free stuff!

If you've enjoyed what you've read, why not tell other people and bag yourself some free stuff in the process?

Simply write a review of this book – or any of the other books in the 'SUCCESS' series – and publicise it via:
- Amazon
- iTunes
- Facebook
- Twitter
- A blog

… or any other online or offline publication.

Then email an image or link to us at hello@nickfox.co.uk.

We'll thank you via Twitter and you'll get back some exclusive property investment tools or samples of our latest materials to help you stay focused and up to date in your investment journey.

Thanks in advance and we hope to hear from you soon!

Some recommended reading

When I mentor clients, I give them a huge list of books I think they should read – some about property, some about the mindset you need to succeed in business and life – so here are the first five of those titles to get you started. You may have already read some of them…in which case, I'd suggest they may be worth a second look!:

Rich Dad, Poor Dad, by Robert T. Kiyosaki
Rich Dad's Cashflow Quadrant, by Robert T. Kiyosaki
The Millionaire Next Door, by Thomas J. Stanley
Wage Slave to Financial Freedom, by Neil Mansell
Think and Grow Rich: The Original Classic, by Napoleon Hill
Goals, by Brian Tracy
Goal Mapping, by Brian Mayne
The Dip, by Seth Godin

Testimonials

For Nick...

"Nick and his team are the real deal. Their knowledge and help in moving my investment project forward has been invaluable. Without their expertise I would not have been able to reach my personal property goals or milestones."
Richard Felton, UK

"Great book, great guy and great results for me after I read 'HMO Property Success'. I've now replaced my job with passive income from HMO properties. Thanks, Nick!"
C.Clark, Bedford

"Nick has clearly got a huge amount of knowledge in his field, and having his support and experience has given me the increased confidence to make my first steps into investing."
Craig Smith, Edinburgh

"Nick is a very experienced property professional. His practical advice on setting goals, the pros and cons of this type of investment and how to minimise risks and properly manage a growing portfolio are essential in what can be a very complex investment. Nick's mentoring is not a get-rich-quick formula but a clear and concise way of demonstrating how a solid property investment strategy can

be put into action. And the results are well worth it."
D. Wright, Aberdeen

"I have spent money in the past on various property courses, where you are taught in a group in a classroom, and those have not really helped me. This one-to-one mentoring with Nick was brilliant, as I was actually seeing his business and properties, meeting tenants, getting lots of advice and seeing what worked well and what didn't in a live situation. I have booked another two days with Nick in my home city next week, to look at various properties and hopefully start my journey as a full-time property investor, and I cannot wait! I highly recommend this type of mentoring!"
James Robinson, Hull

"Both Sarah and I cannot express how much help Nick has been to our property business over the last two years. His support and knowledge have been invaluable. We would thoroughly recommend his mentoring to any budding investor."
Stuart Lewis, Northampton

"Thank you so much for your patience, professionalism and general understanding during our three-day mentoring programme. The visit to see how your office and HMO business runs was incredible and so, so helpful. Without it we would have been at a complete loss. With your guidance and help we have now purchased our first HMO property and look forward to keeping in touch to show you our profitable progress!"
Rebecca Santay-Jones, Harrow

"I first met Nick in the autumn of 2012 when I was looking for someone to guide me through my first HMO purchase. Nick's mentoring was invaluable and gave me such a good grounding - not just in HMOs, but in how to run a successful property business - that I have been able to move forward with real confidence as my business has grown. Even now, if there is something I am uncertain of, or I just want to bounce an idea around, I'm very grateful to have Nick in my corner. He has such wide-ranging experience in the industry and I value his opinion greatly. The income my portfolio already provides gives me the option of going part-time in my day job and in the coming months, as I grow the business further, I fully intend to become a full-time property investor and landlord."

Andy Potter, Fareham

Even more...
...from Nick Fox Property Mentoring.

Thank you for taking the time to read our book; we hope you've found it helpful. If you'd like to extend your knowledge, please check out our website, where you'll find a wealth of free information and details of our mentoring packages.

We offer a range of mentoring options to suit all needs, from short intensive taster sessions to more comprehensive packages that will give you a deeper understanding of property investment and the buy to let market, focusing on the rewards and implications of building an HMO portfolio.

Various choices available include:
- Half-day 'HMO Education and Tour'
- One-day 'Intensive HMO Property Mentoring Course'
- Two-day 'Intensive HMO Property Mentoring Course'
- 12 months' full access to and support from Nick Fox and his Power Team

Whichever package you choose, you can be assured that Nick's commitment to your personal property goals are absolute. Nick and his team get a real kick out of watching others grow their property portfolios by helping them implement the most successful methods that have been tried and tested over many years.

As skilled and experienced professionals, we present our mentoring sessions in such a way that they are easy to understand, while enabling highly effective learning. The acute insights and practical methodology on offer will help you to take your property business to the next level and secure financial independence for you and your loved ones.

Check out our website **www.nickfox.co.uk** or call us on **01908 930369** to find out more.

Find us on FACEBOOK Nick Fox Mentor TWITTER @foxytowers
www.nickfox.co.uk EMAIL hello@nickfox.co.uk TEL 01908 930369
NICK FOX PROPERTY MENTORING
14 Wharfside Bletchley Milton Keynes MK2 2AZ

Read on...

Collect the set of books by Nick Fox to help you achieve financial freedom through property investment.

HMO PROPERTY SUCCESS

Do you want a secure financial future that starts sooner, rather than later as you're approaching retirement? By investing in multi-let properties, you can double or even triple the level of rental income generated by single letting, and realise positive cash flow from the start. In this book, multiple business owner and investor, Nick Fox, clearly guides you through the steps to building an HMO portfolio that delivers both on-going income and a tangible pension or lifestyle pot.

ISBN: 978-0-9576516-0-9
RRP: £9.99

PROPERTY INVESTMENT SUCCESS

How does your financial future look?
If you haven't reviewed your pension provision for a while or aren't completely happy with how your current investments are performing, you should take a closer look at property. In this book, Nick Fox discusses the pros and cons of traditional pensions and makes the case for property as a robust alternative investment vehicle.
He looks at how property can deliver different kinds of returns at different times and shows how you can build a tailored portfolio that perfectly satisfies your own future financial needs.

ISBN: 978-0-9576516-4-7
RRP: £9.99

THE SECRETS OF BUY TO LET SUCCESS

Are you looking for a sound investment that can give you both income and growth on your capital, but nervous about the future of the property market? This book will put your mind at rest. In The Secrets of Buy to Let Success, Nick Fox shares his knowledge and expertise about the market, guiding the reader step by step through the basics of building a solid and profitable property business - even through an economic crisis. If you're completely new to property investment, this book is a great place to start.

ISBN: 978-0-9927817-2-9
RRP: £9.99

101 TOP TIPS FOR PROPERT INVESTMENT SUCCESS

Whether you're looking to focus purely on HMOs, build a varied portfolio of rental properties, or employ a number of different strategies to make money from property, '101 TOP TIPS' is full of useful information that will help keep you at the top of the property investment business.
Nick Fox has spent the past decade amassing a highly profitable buy to let portfolio and continues to invest in a variety of property projects and business ventures. His tailored mentoring programmes have helped many aspiring investors realise their own potential in the property field.

ISBN: 978-0-9935074-9-6 | RRP: £9.99

PROPERTY RENNOVATION & REFURBISHMENT SUCCESS

Successful renovation and refurbishment relies on spending the right amount of money in the right way, so are you ready to hone your budgeting, planning and project-management skills? Alongside the deposit, this is where the biggest chunk of your investment funds will be spent. You need to analyse the figures, budget correctly, plan the work in detail and ensure it's carried out properly so that your buy to let performs as you need it to. Not sure how to do that? Then this is the book for you!

ISBN: 978-0-9927817-6-7
RRP: £11.99

COMPLETE PROPERTY INVESTMENT SUCCESS

This indispensable trilogy takes you through the pros and cons of property as an investment vehicle, looks at the business of buy to let and the different ways you can make money from property, then goes into detail about how to successfully source, refurbish and let out highly cash-positive houses in multiple occupation.

ISBN: 978-0-9927817-0-5
RRP: £26.99

FIRST TIME PROPERTY DEVELOPER

Interested in developing property for profit ? Don't know where to start? Let experienced property expert, Nick Fox, lead you through the process. Nick will show you how to find the property, add genuine value to it by developing and refurbishing and then explain how to sell on for profit or rent out for income.

ISBN: 978-0-9576516-4-7
RRP: £9.99

Available now online at
www.amazon.co.uk & www.nickfox.co.uk
Books, iBook, Kindle & Audio

Find us on FACEBOOK Nick Fox Mentor TWITTER NickFoxPropertyMentoring
www.nickfox.co.uk EMAIL hello@nickfox.co.uk TEL 01908 930369
NICK FOX PROPERTY MENTORING
14 Wharfside Bletchley Milton Keynes MK2 2AZ

Lightning Source UK Ltd.
Milton Keynes UK
UKHW050406110221
378434UK00012B/83